CONTENTS

THE CORPORATE IDENTITY AUDIT

This audit is structured in three parts. Part 1 examines the process of carrying out a corporate identity audit. Part 2 looks at the audit process itself and provides a framework that addresses some of the logistical and process requirements of conducting an audit. Part 3 comprises a series of questions based on the steps in Part 1. These questions are designed to help you plan and implement your audit in a straightforward and practical manner.

The
Corporate
Identity
Audit

A Set of Objective Measurement
Tools for Your Company's Image
and Reputation

Wally Olins
Wolff-Olins Group

Elinor Selame
Brand Equity International

FINANCIAL TIMES
Prentice Hall

An imprint of **PEARSON EDUCATION**

London · New York · San Francisco · Toronto · Sydney
Tokyo · Singapore · Hong Kong · Cape Town · Madrid · Paris · Milan · Munich · Amsterdam

PEARSON EDUCATION LIMITED

Head Office:
Edinburgh Gate
Harlow CM20 2JE
Tel: +44 (0)1279 623623
Fax: +44 (0)1279 431059

London Office:
128 Long Acre, London WC2E 9AN
Tel: +44 (0)207 447 2000
Fax: +44 (0)207 240 5771
Website: www.business-minds.com

First published in Great Britain 2000

© Cambridge Strategy Publications Ltd 2000

Published in association with Cambridge Strategy Publications Ltd
39 Cambridge Place, Cambridge CB2 1NS.

The right of Wally Olins and Elinor Selame to be identified as
Authors of this Work has been asserted by them in accordance
with the Copyright, Design and Patents Act 1988.

ISBN 0 273 64712 1

British Library Cataloguing in Publication Data
A CIP catalogue record for this book can be obtained from the British Library

10 9 8 7 6 5 4 3 2 1

Typeset by Pantek Arts, Maidstone, Kent
Printed and bound in Great Britain

The Publishers' policy is to use paper manufactured from sustainable forests.

INTRODUCTION

Over the last decade, leaders of major companies all over the world have become increasingly concerned about the identity projected by their organization. Identity is an umbrella term that includes both a company's image and its reputation. In a survey conducted by the MORI polling organization in 1992, the chairmen of some of Europe's largest organizations indicated that corporate identity was one of their major concerns. They said that the reputation of a company affects every part of corporate life: share price, recruitment, sales, acquisitions, divestments, and so on. For example, they understood that when a company is well regarded, share price goes up and it is easier to recruit talented people. On the other hand, when the company's reputation suffers, all of these benefits are reversed.

Despite this concern, however, most executives don't know how to place a value on identity. They generally don't know how to manage it. They often don't know why the perception of their company by its audiences improves or gets worse. They may not even comprehend the totality of the elements of which identity consists.

Companies face challenges to their identity from all sides. Some of the factors complicating the establishment of a clear identity include the following:

- Companies are increasingly merging across national boundaries. Corporate leaders have to consider what to do about creating a new corporation with a new identity out of two old and frequently competing organizations with different and sometimes incompatible cultures, as in the case of Brown Boveri and Asea, which merged to become ABB.

- Environmental concerns are becoming increasingly significant, which means that corporate ethical standards have to be inculcated into employees at all locations and organizational levels. One mistake can damage a company for decades, as Exxon discovered with the Valdez disaster.

- Products and services are becoming increasingly similar, which means that consumers make purchases more and more on emotional rather than rational grounds. For example, most consumers would be hard-pressed to identify any real difference between the various kinds of petrol marketed by Shell, British Petroleum, Fina, Elf, or Texaco.

For these and a variety of other reasons, corporate identity is becoming an increasingly important topic in company boardrooms. This audit explains what corporate identity is and what role it plays in determining a company's success or failure. It goes on to describe how the company can assess, monitor and manage its identity.

Identity as a Corporate Resource

In essence, a corporate identity is a major management resource that lets everyone who deals with the organization understand what it is, what it does, and what it aspires to become. In order to understand, develop, and manage its identity, the leaders of an organization must first understand those elements that combine to make up an identity. Next, they must set up a structure that will allow for the development of the identity they want to project. Finally, they must use that structure to monitor and manage that identity. This enables leaders of an organization to harness its identity and use it as a resource. In short, every organization has an identity. Either the organization can control its identity, or the identity will control the organization.

What Is a Corporate Identity?

Regardless of its size, every organization carries out many transactions every day: it buys, it sells, it hires and fires, it makes, it paints, it cleans, it promotes through advertising and other publicity — and so on. In all of these transactions, the organization will in some way be presenting itself — or part of itself — to the various groups of people with whom it deals. The way the company manifests itself, both as a whole and in its separate component parts, will affect the way people feel about it. These various aspects of what a company projects combine to make up its identity. What different audiences perceive is often called the corporate image.

Because the range of corporate activities is so vast and the manifestations of identity so diverse, the corporate identity is not normally managed as a whole unless active steps are taken to do so. Thus, corporate identity can be defined as the *explicit* management of all the ways in which the organization presents itself to all of its audiences. The key word here is *explicit*.

Corporate identity manifests itself in the following areas:

• products and services: what is made or sold

• environments: where products and services are made or sold

• communications: how a company explains what it does

• behavior[*]: the way a company's people represent it to its public

---

[*] It should be noted that behavior, because it cannot be explicitly controlled by a company's management, is sometimes excluded from the definition of corporate identity. Corporate identity experts would agree, however, that the behaviors a company's employees exhibit have a direct bearing on the company's external image.

The four factors are described in detail below.

Products and services. Sometimes a company's products and their performance are the most significant factor in influencing how the organization is perceived. For example, the appearance, performance and price of a BMW product largely influences the way people perceive the company that makes it. A company can specifically design its products, packaging, environments and communications with corporate identity in mind, as in the case of Apple Computer.

Environments. In some organizations, such as leisure centers, hotels and retail stores, the environment is central to maintaining the identity of the organization, as is the case with Holiday Inn or the Amoco Oil Company. In any company, the buildings that house the business tell a corporate story.

By taking a holistic approach, environmental design, vehicles, signing, employee uniforms, etc. can strongly reflect a company's corporate identity if developed and addressed in that manner.

Communications. The formal and informal communications of a company, both to its own staff and to the outside world, influence the way audiences perceive it. In those cases where brands derive their strengths from the totality of the formal communication process (packaging, advertising and so on), formal communication is the most significant way in which the identity emerges. In other words, the public perception of some organizations may be a result of their external communications. An example of a company that uses this source of identity is Coca-Cola.

Behavior. Some organizations, like airlines or police forces or health authorities, derive their identity from the way people who work in those businesses behave. Often the people who most visibly represent the company are at relatively junior levels. Thus, the way customers and others are treated by flight attendants, police, officers etc. often determines how the entire organization will be seen by the public.

In most organizations, however, a combination of all these factors determines the corporate identity as perceived by their audiences.

TYPES OF CORPORATE IDENTITY

The identity of most companies can be divided into three general categories: monolithic, endorsed or branded. The categories are not mutually exclusive, and none is necessarily superior to any of the others. Each is appropriate in specific circumstances. When circumstances change, it may be appropriate to modify identity structures.

Monolithic Identity. This is where the organization uses one name and one visual system throughout all of its interactions. Examples of companies using this strategy include BMW, British Petroleum, Mitsubishi and Sony. Companies with a monolithic identity have usually grown organically, and they may operate in closely related activities. Because everything that the organization with a monolithic identity does

has the same name, style and character, the organization and its products can be clear, consistent and mutually supportive. Figure 1 contains a chart showing the relationships between a company and its divisions using a monolithic structure.

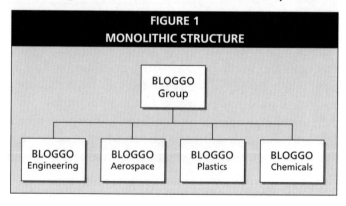

Endorsed Identity. Most companies grow (at least partly) by acquisition, absorbing competitors, suppliers and customers domestically and internationally. Sometimes they find themselves with a multiplicity of brands. The acquiring company is often eager to preserve the goodwill (equity) associated with these acquisitions, but at the same time to superimpose its own management style and reward systems on the

subsidiaries or partners. Under an endorsed identity strategy, the parent keeps some or all of the names and styles of its acquisitions, but endorses these with the corporate name and visual style. Figure 2 shows the relationship between a parent and its divisions, given an endorsed structure.

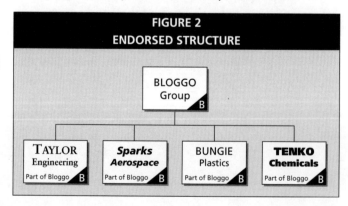

Both United Technologies and, increasingly, Nestlé have used this approach. These companies, which are often complex multi-sector businesses, also need to impress financial and other audiences with their size, strength and sense of direction. Therefore, they need to emphasize both diversity and consistency simultaneously. These paradoxical aims can be achieved simultaneously provided that the corporation and its subsidiaries understand and are sensitive to the issues involved in this complexity and are prepared to deal with them honestly and consistently.

Branded Identity. Some companies, especially those in consumer products, separate their corporate identity from the identities of the brands and companies they own, as is the case with Unilever, American Home Products, and Reckitt & Colman. So far as

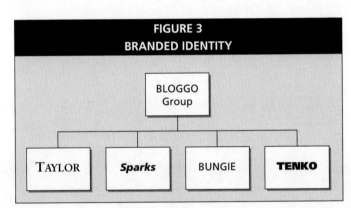

FIGURE 3
BRANDED IDENTITY

BLOGGO
Group

TAYLOR   *Sparks*   BUNGIE   **TENKO**

the final consumer is concerned, the corporation does not exist. What the customer identifies with is the brand. Brands have names, reputations, life cycles, and personalities of their own, and they may even compete with other brands from the same company. When this approach is used, the corporation's identity is aimed at all of its audiences except the final consumer, and brand identities are aimed only at the final consumer. Figure 3 illustrates this approach.

Management Disciplines and Corporate Identity

The management disciplines embraced by the corporate identity program include corporate strategy, marketing, communications, organizational behavior, and increasingly finance, which places an asset value on the equity of a company's corporate and/or brand identities.

The fundamental idea behind a corporate identity program is that all of these disciplines are explicitly managed for a particular purpose. The purpose of a corporate identity program is to project a clear idea of what the organization is, what it does, what it stands for, and where it is going.

In short, the organization has to manage the way its products and services look, behave and communicate, if it is to develop a clear corporate identity.

THE ROLE OF VISION IN CORPORATE IDENTITY

Most companies develop an identity that emerges naturally as part of what they are. Often the identity is a manifestation of the personality of the founder of the business; such identities are often characterized by their informality. The company's behavior patterns, its communications and the appearance of its products, services, offices and showrooms, are a result of the influence of a few people, usually the founders and certain influential people within the industry. There comes a time when this casual, uncultivated identity is no longer appropriate. Reasons for re-examining corporate identity include the following:

- The requirement for a re-assessment of the corporate identity may arise because of a merger, diversification, reorganization or other structural, strategic or management change.

- It may be required because there is consistent evidence that the outside world misunderstands and undervalues the corporation, or that there is insufficient internal co-ordination and unity.

- An ever more important reason for approaching corporate identity with consistency is that as corporations grow, expand, diversify and internationalize, there is usually no single message about what the company is and what it stands for.

- Competition between the world's most successful companies is no longer confined to the products and services they make. The best companies all make outstanding products. If consumers can't distinguish between competing products rationally, they will increasingly choose between them on the basis of their emotional reactions to the products or to the company itself. Mercedes-Benz and BMW cars are technically very similar, as are hamburgers from McDonald's and Burger King. Many customers would react quite differently to each of the two companies in these pairs, however. This comparability of products and services applies in an increasing number of industries, including banking, financial services, oil, chemicals, computers, cars, etc.

- As companies expand their global marketing activities, economies of scale must be sought. Successful corporate identity management can help reduce operating expenses when design systems are developed which can be easily implemented internationally.

Formal efforts to manage corporate identity often grow out of a combination of all of these factors. As emotional factors become more important in distinguishing between organizations whose products may not be unique, the corporate vision becomes more significant. The corporate vision — who we are, what we do, how we do it, and what we want to become. This vision helps others to answer related questions: Why should I buy from or work for this company? Why should I collaborate with this company or buy shares of its stock? At the same time, the corporate identity of the organization is increasingly becoming the vehicle by which the vision is communicated to all of a company's audiences. A company needs to consider formalizing and actively managing its corporate identity when it becomes clear that there are significant gaps between the reality of the organization and the way it is perceived either internally or externally.

Audiences

The audiences of an organization are those people who come into contact with it at any time, in any place, and in any form of relationship. It is often assumed that the most important audience for any company is its customers. However, there are many groups of people working in and around an organization who will have contact with it. Some of these are listed below:

Internal and quasi-internal audiences

• All staff, at all levels, in all companies and divisions, in all countries

• Directors

• Families of employees

• Pensioners

• Representatives of trade unions

• Shareholders

External audiences

• Central government, local government, regional government

• Competitors

• Customers, both direct and indirect

• Investment analysts, bankers, stockbrokers

- Journalists

- Opinion leaders

- Potential recruits

- Schools and universities

- Suppliers

- Trade and industry associations

These audiences are not always separate and independent. To some extent they are overlapping. Pensioners and journalists may also be customers. Customers may also be shareholders, and so on. Different audiences will form a view of an organization based on the totality of the impressions that the company makes on them. When these impressions are contradictory — where impressions made in one place are different from those made somewhere else — the overall impression will be confusing at best and negative at worst.

INTRODUCING CORPORATE IDENTITY AS A PRIORITY

The biggest difficulty in introducing identity management as a resource is getting it into the corporate bloodstream. Unless people within the organization at every level accept the corporate vision and are prepared to integrate it into every part of the corporate system with which they are associated, it will crumble. The importance and potential role of an identity management system can be best described by comparing it to other systems already functioning in the organization. Perhaps the two most significant and appropriate role models to help people throughout the organization think about identity management are financial management and information technology management, both of which are accepted as standard resources in successful institutions.

Financial Management. Financial management, with all of its rites and rituals, such as annual, monthly and even weekly forecasting, budgeting, reporting and accounting, as well as the web of people permeating the organization, is so much a part of every corporate undertaking that its role is accepted without question. The corporate financial system is seen as being legitimate throughout every part of the organization. No subsidiary or branch, however independent or remote, is ever permitted to run its own financial systems according to its own rules, or to operate without effective financial management systems in place.

Information Technology Management. Information technology management is beginning to play a role similar to that of financial systems within organizations, although its presence is not yet as widely or completely felt. Within a generation, first the computer itself and then a complex network of information technology systems have become a significant corporate resource. An entire function has developed around assessing, satisfying and managing the organization's information needs. No part of the organization is immune from the influence of information technology systems. All parts of the organization are linked by them. Information Technology systems and their management are part of the corporate way of being. No part of the corporation can unilaterally abdicate from the system and survive in today's business world.

Identity management, like financial management and information technology management, must cut across all of the conventional corporate structures and influence every part of the company if it is to be successful and become integrated in a way that will produce the intended benefits. Only in this way will the organization be able to realize the full impact of effectively managing its identity.

When to Introduce a Corporate Identity Program

As previously stated, most companies will reach a point where a corporate identity program becomes a necessity. This point may be precipitated by factors such as mergers, privatization, diversification, major investment or divestment, problems that arise from a lack of internal cohesion or from misunderstandings about the nature of the organization. This generally is the result of a lack of a clear corporate vision. This will prompt company leaders to focus on projecting a coherent identity to all of the audiences with whom it deals.

The first step in addressing these problems is to assess the company's current identity. Below are some steps that will result in data about how an organization's current identity compares with the message the company wants to communicate to its various audiences. This process will help the leaders of an organization determine whether or not a formal identity program is needed, and what direction that program should take if it is developed. The audit steps are followed by an outline of the basic elements required to launch a successful corporate identity program.

STEPS IN PERFORMING AN IDENTITY AUDIT

Although it is unlikely that an organization will be able to carry out a major identity program with internal resources alone, it is possible and desirable for the organization to examine and audit its own identity in order to determine what further work may be required. The following steps provide an overview of an audit that can be carried out internally.

Step 1: Select the Audit Team

The audit team must have enough influence to ensure that corporate identity is seen as an important issue throughout the organization. The audit team may consist of individuals with expertise in sales and marketing, communications, operations, construction management, engineering and design. The team composition will vary depending upon the nature of the company.

Step 2: Assess Key Elements in the Corporate Identity

The audit team must be clear about the nature of the organization, the key components of its corporate identity, and the ways in which they are projected.

Step 3: Determine Who Should Be Interviewed

Data must be gathered from a variety of sources both inside and outside the company.

Step 4: Conduct Audit Interviews

The research phase of the audit involves both interviewing and systematically examining the physical representations of the company's identity.

Step 5: Audit Corporate Identity Factors

Additional assessments are now used to establish the level of consistency between different departments or divisions.

Step 6: Summarize Salient Points

During the interviews, certain critical and consistent points will emerge. These will enable auditors to uncover important issues in assessing the corporate identity, and will lead to consensus-building within the organization.

Step 7: Determine the Options for Change

The audit team should explore the differences between how the company is perceived by various audiences and how it would like it to be perceived.

Step 8: Present the Audit Results

The development of an effective corporate identity program will rest on the effectiveness of presenting the findings of the audit.

Step 9: Use the Audit Data to Improve the Corporate Identity

Most companies fail to manage their identity actively and effectively. This audit concludes by providing ideas for using the identity as a powerful management tool.

SELECT THE AUDIT TEAM

R aising questions about the corporate identity is usually unsettling to staff and outsiders alike. It is important to keep this in mind while in the process of completing the audit. An effective audit calls for the creation of a small, influential team. Possible team members may include senior level executives and/or middle managers with expertise in sales and marketing, marketing research, communications, operations, engineering and industrial and graphic design.

It is important to note that the corporate identity audit team members may be segmented into smaller interview groups to expedite the process and to pair appropriate levels, backgrounds and expertise with each intended audience/group/individual being interviewed. These people should operate in a way that is unthreatening and unobtrusive.

The scope of work carried out by the team can best be described as follows:

• Investigate how the company is perceived.

• Determine why the company is perceived in this way.

• Agree (if possible) on how the company should be perceived.

• Decide how to create that perception.

The first job for the team is to prepare a written brief that describes the task. This should be comprehensive and take into account its parameters in terms of strategy, marketing, communication and behavior. A short version of this brief should be circulated to senior and middle management who will, where appropriate, cascade it down to their own departments. A variation should also be circulated to selected external audiences.

Below is an example of what this brief, which should be signed by the CEO, might look like:

> *We are currently examining how clearly the activities of the company and its component parts are understood by our own staff and by those with whom we come into contact, such as suppliers, customers, financial audiences and so on. Because of this concern, I have asked a small team to explore this issue. If any member of the team contacts you, I would be grateful if you would give them your co-operation. Naturally, all discussions will be confidential.*

Once the brief has been distributed, the team can begin its work, which will consist primarily of interviewing appropriate individuals inside and outside the company. This work is described below.

ASSESS KEY ELEMENTS IN THE CORPORATE IDENTITY

Elements of the Corporate Identity

Before undertaking a corporate identity audit, senior management needs to be clear about the context in which that identity operates. This will help to focus the subsequent audit and resulting identity program.

The first assessment should consider the four areas in which corporate identity manifests itself. This can be conducted by the audit team and relates to the descriptions on pages 4-5.

Considering the company's main products and services, its location and physical environment, the way it communicates, and its people, the team should assess the importance of each category in shaping the corporate identity.

In completing this assessment, most attention should normally be paid to the perceptions of customers and/or the general public. Shareholder perceptions, for example, will largely be based on financial performance and these should be excluded from this assessment; however, factors shaping the perceptions of financial analysts will need to be considered. For some companies, the way the organization is presented on television and in the press may define public perceptions. In this case, attention must be paid to the factors that influence the thinking of journalists about the company.

A sample assessment form is shown below.

Rate the importance of each of the following factors in shaping the way people perceive your organization. For each factor use a scale of 0-10, where 0 = no significance and 10 = critically important.

The company's products and services themselves. Includes all goods and services used and paid for by customers. BMW rates high on this scale.

The company's environment. Includes its location, building, external and internal appearance. Holiday Inn rates high on this scale.

The company's communications. Includes all formal and informal communications, notably advertising, public awareness programs, media presentations and all company literature. Coca Cola rates high on this scale.

Behavior. This should emphasize the perceived and actual behavior of all uniformed staff or employees bearing clear corporate identification such as hats and name tags when in contact with the public/customers. Any police force rates high on this scale.

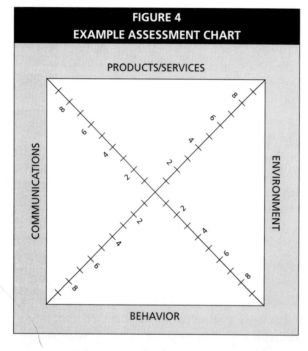

FIGURE 4
EXAMPLE ASSESSMENT CHART

PRODUCTS/SERVICES

COMMUNICATIONS

ENVIRONMENT

BEHAVIOR

Plot each figure on the chart in Figure 4 and shade as shown.

A completed example is shown in Figure 5 for a company scoring:

• Products and services: 3

• Environment: 8

• Communications: 5

• Behavior: 0

Type of Corporate Identity

Senior management should also be clear about the type of identity which the organization possesses. Again, this will help to focus the subsequent audit and resulting identity program.

This second assessment should consider the three main categories of corporate identity. This assessment can also be conducted by the audit team itself and with reference to the definitions given on pages 6-7.

Considering the company's name, brands, advertising strategy, competition, presence in different international markets, and referring to the definitions given above, the team should assess the importance of each category in the company's overall identity.

FIGURE 5
COMPLETED EXAMPLE ASSESSMENT CHART

PRODUCTS/SERVICES

COMMUNICATIONS

ENVIRONMENT

BEHAVIOR

In completing this assessment, most attention should again be paid to the perceptions of customers and/or the general public, since the financial community will inevitably have a stronger awareness of the corporate whole than of individual brands.

A sample assessment form is shown below.

Rate each of the following categories as they apply to your organization. For each factor use a scale of 0-10, where 0 = no relevance and 10 = perfect definition. The three scores must add up to 10.

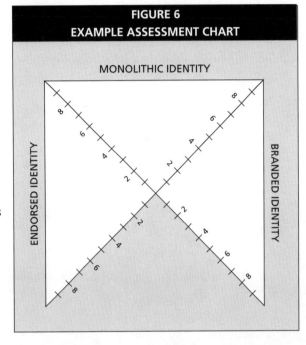

FIGURE 6
EXAMPLE ASSESSMENT CHART

Monolithic identity. Everything that the organization makes or does has the same name, style and character. Sony rates high on this scale.

Endorsed identity. There is an umbrella name and a general consistency of approach, but individual divisions, brands or businesses retain their identity. Nestlé rates high on this scale.

Branded identity. As far as the consumer is concerned, each brand, division or business is entirely separate. The company is effectively invisible. Unilever rates high on this scale.

Plot each figure on the chart in Figure 6 and shade as shown.

Note that a more complex breakdown of the types of corporate identity is shown in Figure 12. It may be helpful to refer to that section now, if the assessment form proves difficult to complete.

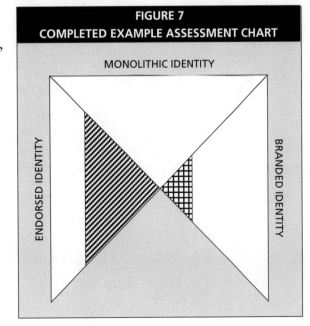

FIGURE 7
COMPLETED EXAMPLE ASSESSMENT CHART

A completed example is shown in Figure 7 for a company scoring:

- Monolithic identity: 0

- Endorsed identity: 7

- Branded identity: 3

DETERMINE WHO SHOULD BE INTERVIEWED

In a very large, diversified, international organization it will not be possible to select a statistically significant sample that will be representative of every element that deals with the organization. It is not even desirable to attempt this. The main purpose of this stage of the audit is to gain insight into whether there is a consensus view either internally or externally about the organization. Secondly, this stage of the audit will reveal whether there is any significant discrepancy between internal and external perceptions. Finally, the audit provides an excellent opportunity to uncover real or political issues which may either enhance the development of, or inhibit the acceptance and implementation of, a corporate identity program.

The audit team should be receptive to "gems" of information they may uncover about the company, including suggestions and opportunities which may be outside the realm of corporate identity. They should also be aware of the political sensitivity and confidentiality of the information which is shared or discussed.

Each audit — internal and external — usually requires that about 30 people be interviewed, although the number will vary according to the size of the company, the number of its units and their diversity.

Internal Interviews

Although the interview program is not intended to be statistically significant it should be representative. It is important to cut "a diagonal slice" through the organization, that is to say, select interviewees from all levels and all parts of the company. In addition, care should be taken that interviewees are an appropriate demographic mix; that they reasonably represent the age/sex/profile of the company.

In most nationally-based companies, 20-30 people should be sufficient as a base, but in organizations with many divisions and overseas operations the number might be doubled or even trebled to get a reasonable mix. Normally, the heads of each division should be interviewed, along with an appropriate number of middle managers and staff.

The role of the audit team in selecting potential interviewees is to ensure that undue weight is not given to any particular area of the business. There may be political reasons why some internal audiences are included as interviewees. It will also be important to include a small number of interviewees who have worked for the company for a relatively short time (say 6-24 months).

External Interviews

Interviews should be conducted, again with around 30 people representing journalists, suppliers, competitors, collaborators and customers. (Refer to the list on pages 10-11 to ensure that no significant group has been excluded). In the case of external interviewees, it is not necessary to seek people with a very close working knowledge of the organization. A detached view will be more representative of the wider audience for which the selected interviewees speak.

As before, the role of the audit team in selecting interviewees must be to ensure a balance. For example, customers should be chosen at random, not from a list of "best customers" or from a list of those that have recently written to the company. In this context, it may be worth talking to the customers of competitors, to find out why they don't buy from the firm whose identity is being audited.

The list of interviewees, both internal and external, should be compiled and cross-checked by different members of the team, canvassing amongst their senior colleagues.

At this stage, and later, interviewees should be given only the most general idea of the purpose of the interview, which should always be referred to in terms of "research", rather than as an audit. The brief, described on page 17, should be sufficient introduction. However, it may be necessary to reassure some internal interviewees that their responses will not be attributed to them individually but rather documented collectively. Further, their answers will not be taken in any way to reflect upon their current performance or future prospects. In short, it should be made clear that there are no right or wrong answers, and that the interviews are confidential.

Conduct Audit Interviews

Once the list of people to be interviewed is completed, the audit team is ready to begin its research. Each interview should last from 30 to 60 minutes in length. In some cases, a second or follow-up interview may be necessary. This section describes methods to be used in that research, and suggests some of the results that auditors might expect to find in the course of the research.

The main objective of the interviews will be to establish:

• how much people know about the company.

• what opinions or judgments they attach to their knowledge of the company.

• how clear and consistent those opinions and judgments are.

• how far those opinions and judgments vary from the identity which senior managers wish to project.

For both internal and external interviewees, the range of questions should cover the four areas of corporate identity: products/services, environments, communications, and behavior. In addition, the following issues, in roughly the order shown, should be addressed in the course of the interview:

Nature of the industry/sector in which the organization operates

Issues to be covered here include industry/sector size, growth patterns, rates of change, competitiveness, use of technology, environmental concerns, corporate culture, and profitability.

The organization itself

Issues to be covered here include size, position, profitability, market share, competitiveness, quality, advertising, and environmental responsibility.

Brands, businesses and divisions [see page 20]

Here the interviews seek to establish whether the internal perception of the *type* of corporate identity is matched in reality by external perceptions.

Lists of sample questions appear in Figures 8, 9 and 10.

Internal Interviews

The responses from the internal interviews will be influenced less by confusion than by attitude. Although insiders will know much more about the organization than outsiders, they will be far more emotionally involved with it. Their responses may be heavily conditioned by their role, responsibility, and length of service with the company.

Each internal group will have a view (often inflated) of its own significance in the organization and each will have a view on the competence, loyalty and roles of all the other divisions, brands, services, or of the corporation as a whole. All the divisions will have a view of the center, either favorable, unfavorable, or, more likely, mixed. The following are typical responses from internal interviews: "They don't understand the problems of our division; Head office has no understanding of marketing; They are obsessed with and dominated by financial matters; How can you expect us to perform properly if we are run by accountants?"

When interview questions address the issue of the company identity directly, representatives from some divisions may say that controlling their own name and image is vital to success in their markets, and that the corporation will have to allow them this freedom if they are to succeed. People at the center will have their own perspective on the loyalty, ability and significance of each division. "If you look at our organization, it's clear that division A is a core activity and it knows it, while division B is a collection of companies which we will eventually have to get rid of. There is no common quality level among any of their businesses and none of them adds anything to the group except turnover!"

The center will also be concerned with independent baronies and fiefdoms. Central co-ordinating resources like personnel, finance, information technology, research and development and communication will all have views on their significance to the organization. Each group will also have an opinion about the attitude of the different divisions and groups towards it. Newer acquisitions will express different views from older businesses. Nationals of the "home country" of the company may have views that differ from their counterparts in other lands.

Internal Interviewing Techniques

Opinions about all of these issues should emerge from the interviewing process. It follows, then, that interviews should be informal, confidential, and loosely structured. Although interviewers must be clear about the issues to be dealt with, they should be careful not to follow a set written questionnaire too closely.

Figure 8 lists the main issues which should be addressed in each interview and suggests possible questions that are designed to elicit accurate answers. Note that these questions should be tailored to suit the particular make-up, market and operating environment of the company.

As in the sample questions below, it will be necessary to retain a balance of closed and open questions. Closed questions, which can be answered with a simple "yes", "no" or similar statement, will help to put the interviewee at ease and collect information that can be compared accurately. Open questions, which will provoke more complex, opinion-based answers, may lead the interviewer into new and unsuspected areas. Interesting issues should be fully explored — hence the need not to follow the questionnaire too rigorously.

The interviewer should start by explaining that the meeting is part of a research project and that this, together with all the other interviews, is confidential. Questions should then get on to a personal note:

• How long have you been with the company?

• What did you do before?

This "warm-up" part of the meeting is important.

• because it enables both parties to begin to get to know each other.

• because it gives interviewees a sense of their own significance.

• because it enables the interviewer to get some idea of the person being questioned.

After these preliminaries, the interviewer should say: "I know that your job title is x but can you help me understand what your areas of responsibility include and how you support or relate to other departments or divisions within the company?" At this point there is a real possibility that the respondent will start to open up.

The interviewer, who will of course guide the session, should not discourage a stream of anecdotes and unstructured reminiscences. The object is to gain the confidence of the interviewee so that all the issues are discussed quite freely and without reserve or caution. If this involves going over the same ground a few times it doesn't necessarily matter. The tone of the meeting should be cordial, confidential and informal. The interviewing structure should exist in the interviews but not get in the way.

It sometimes pays for the interviewer to be challenging or act as devil's advocate. For example:

• "I understand that the company is run by a strong CEO. Do you believe the CEO should have more or less control and why?"

• "Besides the CEO or chairman, who else is known for making key decisions?

• "What is the company especially good at and is this well-known to outside audiences? Is it good at marketing or manufacturing or cost control? In what areas does the company need improvement and is this well-known to outside audiences?"

• "Which is the best company in the whole business? I mean which of your competitors do you most fear?"

FIGURE 8

SUGGESTED QUESTIONS FOR THE CORPORATE IDENTITY AUDIT INTERNAL INTERVIEW

1. How long have you been with the company?
2. What did you do before you worked here?
3. What is your position/responsibility in the company?
4. Have your perceptions of the company changed since you began to work here?
   What were your perceptions before working here?
   What are they now?
5. What image attributes would you associate with your company?

Innovative	Friendly	Progressive	Formal
Conservative	Futuristic	Dependable	Trustworthy
National/Regional/International		Responsive	

6. How would you describe your company and its products/services to friends or strangers who asked?
7. In your opinion, is your company understood by outsiders as you understand it? If not, what is the difference in the way outside people view the organization?
8. How would you describe the products and services your company offers to someone in your industry?
9. Who do you believe are your company's major competitors? Please rank 1, 2, 3, etc.
10. Do you see an opportunity for your own personal growth with the company? Why or why not?
11. Where do you see the company's opportunities for growth? How? Why?
12. What barriers are preventing the company from achieving the growth you described?
13. What is your opinion of the current corporate identity used by the company?
14. What does the current symbol/signature/trademark suggest to you? Do you think it reflects the personality and long-term mission of the company? Why or why not?
15. What colors do you associate with the company?
16. What are the major strengths and weaknesses of the company in general, i.e., what does the company do best?
17. What are the major strengths and weaknesses of the products/services of the company?
18. If there were one important message you wanted to deliver to the CEO of the company, what would that be?
19. In what ways do you think the company could communicate better to its diverse publics?

Brands:

20. It is my understanding that each brand manager runs his/her own area. Do you believe this structure is appropriate today? Should they have more or less autonomy and why?
21. What visual relationship should the company's branded products and services have to the parent company or division?

External Interviews

The responses from external interviews are likely to show a much greater divergence of knowledge about the company, while they will be less influenced by opinions of a particular department or key employee. Outsiders will also be likely to have a more two-dimensional view of the organization and be less aware of conflicts, politics, and subtleties of approach and be less emotional than internal interviewees.

The purpose of these interviews will be to find out how much outsiders know about the mechanics of the company (size, profitability, ownership and its primary products, services, and divisions); what their views are about its strengths, weaknesses and impact on the outside world; and what image attributes and overall perceptions they have about the organization.

Each group of outsiders (customers, financial analysts, suppliers, etc.) is likely to know more about those topics that directly concern them, or have stronger opinions about different topics. But even in the financial world, where analysts are paid to dissect a company's structure and performance, there is a great deal of misunderstanding and misinformation. In the outside world in general, among customers, opinion leaders, government officials and so on, there is often considerable variation in opinions, perceptions and levels of understanding about a company.

Depending on the audit team's evaluations at Step 2, the questions will need to take close account of the different types of corporate identity and the key factors at work. First, the questions should check whether external perceptions of, say, the importance of brands and staff behavior match the perceptions of the internal interviewees. Second, the questions should establish in greater detail the interviewee's feelings and opinions on these factors. Questions should necessarily be weighted towards the most important factors. If a company is largely perceived in terms of its communications with the public, there will be little point in asking detailed questions about its environment.

External Interviewing Techniques

As with internal interviews, it is important to adopt a flexible structure for the interview with a good mix of open and closed questions. It may, however, be necessary to direct external interviewees more carefully if there is a tendency to focus too much on a single advertisement, customer experience or other "atypical event".

Figure 9 suggests sample interview questions which would be suitable for customers, suppliers, the general public and journalists. Figure 10 presents more in-depth and business-related areas of discussion for financial analysts and outside consultants such as the company's advertising agency or public relations firm.

As in the case of all interviews, it should be recognised that face-to-face interviews increase the risk of bias in the response because individuals may be unwilling to express hostile or critical feelings openly. If such bias is suspected or anticipated, it may be helpful to conduct the interview by telephone, or to use a preliminary telephone interview before conducting face-to-face questioning.

FIGURE 9

SUGGESTED QUESTIONS FOR THE CORPORATE IDENTITY AUDIT EXTERNAL INTERVIEW (SUPPLIERS, GENERAL PUBLIC)

1. What is your relationship to company *x*?
2. How familiar would you say you are with company *x*? (prompt: very familiar, somewhat familiar, not at all familiar)
3. How would you describe what company *x* does? What specific brand name products/ services does it offer?
4. Do you believe the company is a regional, national or international organization?
5. Who do you believe are the primary competitors of company *x*?
6. Based on your own experiences or based on what you have heard or read, would you rate company *x*'s overall reputation as excellent, good, fair or poor?
7. When you hear the name of company *x*, what things come to mind?
8. Why do you do business with company *x*?
9. Would you recommend this company's products/services to a friend? Why or why not?
10. Can you recall or describe any advertising the company has done recently? How did it influence your perception of the company?
11. Could you recognize the company's annual report among others on a crowded coffee table?
12. What symbol and colors come to mind when you hear the company's name?
13. What words (image attributes) would you use to describe the company?
    Innovative   Friendly   Progressive   Formal
    Conservative   Futuristic   Dependable   Trustworthy
    National/Regional/International   Responsive
14. If the company came out with a new product or service, would you/your own company be a primary sales target? If so, why?
15. How would you rate this company's products/services on a scale of one to five when compared to the competition?
16. How would this company's products be viewed in other countries in terms of product quality and image, on a scale of one to five, five being high quality and image; one being low quality and image?
17. Is it important for you to know the company who makes the branded products and services you buy? Do you think the company's name should be clearly communicated along with the brand name?
18. How would you rate the company's sales literature in presenting an image that is clear and consistent with the company's desired positioning?

Keep in mind that external audiences generally have less time to spend in an interview than the company's employees. The suggested length — which should be stated upfront when scheduling the interview — is 15-20 minutes. For this reason, the

FIGURE 10

SUGGESTED QUESTIONS FOR THE CORPORATE IDENTITY AUDIT EXTERNAL INTERVIEW
(FINANCIAL ANALYSTS AND OUTSIDE CONSULTANTS)

Nature of the industry

1. Is it a high growth/low growth industry?
2. Is it going through rapid technological/marketing development or is it stable?
3. Is it, or will it become, highly competitive?
4. Is it converging into a few groups?
5. Is it threatened by environmental or other external considerations?
6. Is it intrinsically a capital/labor-intensive business?

The company

7. Is the company well positioned/badly positioned in the market place?
8. How big is its market share?
9. How profitable is it?
10. How many people does it employ?
11. Is the employment vs profitability figure good or bad by industry standards?
12. Who are its main competitors?
13. How does each of the major players compare in terms of:
    — size?
    — profitability?
    — geographic spread?
    — product range?
    — product quality?
    — innovation/technology?
    — marketing?
    — public image?
    — known brand names?
14. What is the long-term vision of the company?
15. Is the management good enough to execute it?
16. On the whole has the business improved or deteriorated in the last five years? What sort of business will it be in 5 years' time?
17. Will it occupy its present position, or will it be stronger/weaker?
18. Is there an admired model within the industry?
19. Who is it?
20. How is it better/worse than our company in terms of:
    — marketing?
    — technology?
    — sales?
    — product quality?
    — service?
    — distribution?
21. What makes it the admired model?
    — image?
    — long history in the market?
    — market share?

Brands

22. Is the company known mainly through its corporate name — or its brand names?
23. What are the main brand names?
24. Do most respondents know most brand names or are most people only familiar with the brands with which they deal?
25. How does the company articulate the relationship between brand names and corporate names?

interview questionnaire should be tailored to elicit the most salient points desired from each interview group. The main objective is to determine the image perceptions these individuals hold about the company and the degree to which their cumulative opinions are consistent or inconsistent with those of the company's internal publics and senior management.

AUDIT CORPORATE IDENTITY FACTORS

Step 2 of this audit required an assessment of the key elements of the corporate identity. Specifically, it assessed how important products/services, environment, communication and behavior were to the overall identity.

The relative weightings allocated in Step 2 to each of these factors will have been confirmed or revised as a result of the internal and external interviews. These interviews will also produce a cross-section of opinion on the way that the organization projects itself in each of these four areas.

Now the audit team needs to conduct an independent review of these elements. This review can take place at the same time as the interviews. It is essential that a talented and professional designer serve on the audit team which evaluates all visual communications.

Products, Services and Environment

The audit team should review all pertinent items from the corporate identity checklist below and assemble the appropriate samples from each department, division, unit or site. It should also collect products or packaging materials, where appropriate.

Corporate Identity Checklist

Proposals
Billheads
Letterheads
Business cards
Envelopes
Advertising formats
Promotional items
Internal publications
Memo forms
Labels on packages, letters, etc.
Shipping containers
Gummed tape
Name plates
Embossing dies and stamps used on products
Rubber stamps for check endorsement, mail receiving, etc.
Production and cost control forms

Master forms
Name tags
Press release letterheads
Vehicles

At the same time, the team should visit, and photograph if necessary, different buildings, sites, showrooms, stores and offices. Attention should be paid to both the internal and the external appearance.

Different organizations will have other ways of projecting their identity visually. These may include staff uniforms, extensive use of the company logo, the design and colour of delivery vehicles. Examples or photographs of all appropriate symbols should be collected, reviewed and checked for coherence in visual presentation and quality. This collection should be carefully catalogued to highlight inconsistencies, which may be considerable.

Some of the questions to be asked in this phase include:

• Is there a graphic standards program in place for the current corporate identity program?

• Is the design quality consistent with the quality standards and image the company wishes to project?

• Are there ways to reduce the costs of elements bearing the corporate identity, such as eliminating duplicate communications, consolidating sizes, increasing volume orders, new ways to use technology, etc.?

• Would implementing a new corporate identity in phases bring about lower or higher costs than implementing the program at once?

For example, it is interesting to note here that an American Utility Company, Public Service of Colorado, concluded after an in-depth study that the estimated five-year savings after expenses of a phased-in program would be more than $600,000.

This survey will highlight how the various parts of the organization fit together. However, the team should be careful not to pursue consistency for consistency's sake. Significant variations in the appearance of two types of publicity material will be important if both are seen by the same audience. If the two sets of materials are never seen by the same customer or audience, then the discrepancy will be less important. In terms of the corporate identity system, however, it should be noted that consistency in design and execution is the most cost-effective approach.

FIGURE 11
CORPORATE COMMUNICATIONS CHECKLIST

Documents and Instruments

Corporate
  Articles of Incorporation
  Corporate seals
  Stock certificate
Other
  Sales, Purchase, Service, and Utility contracts
  Licenses
  Deeds and Leases
  Mortgages
  Powers of attorney
  Certificates of title
  Securities in Company Portfolio (registration)
  Easements

Office and Production Supplies and Equipment

Business cards
Check signing machine
Decals
Printed containers or wrappers
  Cartons and crates
  Wrapping paper, foil
Interoffice stationery
Invoices
Purchase order forms
Acknowledgements
Labels
Books of account
Letterheads
Envelopes
All standard forms
Plates
  Postage-meter slugs
  Check-endorsing slugs
Rubber stamps
Shipping papers
Engraved machinery/tools
Vehicles

Permits and Licenses

Vending
Hazardous materials, gasoline
Vehicle registration
Building or equipment
  Inspection certificates
  Elevator
  Boiler

Employees

Club name
Club membership cards
Identity cards, badges, passes
Instruction manuals, handbooks, films
Service certificates, awards
Uniforms, athletic clothing
Employee benefit plan forms
Employee recruiting literature
Policy Manual
Safety Manual

Advertising and Promotion

Corporate Identity Manual
Signs and emblems
  Window lettering
  Street and roadside
  On plants, office buildings, and warehouses
Lobby and showroom displays
Gift inventories — calendars, pens, pencils, etc.
Publications
  Pamphlets
  Manuals
  House organs
  Magazines
  Catalogs
  News Release
Newspaper advertisements
Television advertisements
Direct Mail
Posters
Merchandising aid
Giveaways

Literature

News release
Annual report
Quarterly report
Capabilities and services brochure
Catalog cover/pages
New pages for catalog
Public relations information
Sales bulletin
"Literature You Requested"
Newsletter

Films and videotapes

Trademarks and copyrights

Internal Notification

Subsidiaries/associates
Branch offices
Plants
Factory distribution centers
All employees

External Notification

Customers
Government agencies
Building agencies
Foreign
Commissions/authorities
Financial Organizations
  Banks
  Insurance companies
  Stock exchanges
  Stock transfer agent(s)
  Credit agencies
  Underwriters
Post offices
Shareholders
  Financial analysts
  Suppliers
Transportation companies
  Shippers and forwarders
  Railways, airlines etc.
Utility companies
  Communications
  Yellow Page listings/ads
  Electricity and gas
Service organizations
  Credit unions
  Group health services
  Hotels
  Private security policies
Distributors
  Wholesalers and retailers
Publishers of directories
Trade associations
Chamber of Commerce
Civic groups
Clubs/groups where membership is paid by the company
General public announcements
Labor unions

Communication

At the same time, the audit team should consider how the organization deals with its own audiences through public relations, annual reports, display and TV advertising, and other formal and informal channels (see the corporate communications checklist in Figure 11). Does the group always describe itself consistently? Does a coherent message emerge? Is there a clear organizational chart and is the company's structure reflected properly in the corporate identity and visual communications material put forth? Should it be?

Additional questions which may be asked in this context include:

Internal communications

• How does the organization communicate with its employees and, where appropriate, with other quasi-internal audiences?

• Does it have regular videos or newsletters?

• How many?

• How often?

• Aimed at which audiences?

• Controlled by whom?

• Are these top down or bottom up?

• Is the general quality good or poor?

Media

As part of the audit process, the technical and general media should be reviewed in order to see how the group and its activities are perceived.

• What do TV and the press say about the company?

• How often is it in the news and in what context?

• What formal and informal media and public relations activities does it undertake?

• Are these controlled centrally or by division?

- What is the relationship between brands and corporate communications?

- What is the relationship between marketing, advertising, and corporate communication departments?

Behavior

Here the audit team may already have access to a considerable body of survey material in the form of customer opinion/satisfaction research. If such surveys are not conducted regularly, or recent results are not available, then a customer survey program should be instituted. (See the Customer Satisfaction Audit in this Portfolio). Alternatively, the audit team may wish to include additional questions in existing survey/opinion-gathering forms and questionnaires.

In this part of the audit, it will be important to remember that it is consistency which is being measured. Customer Satisfaction surveys, however, will pay more attention to improvement or deterioration in reported perceptions of employee behavior. For this reason, the Corporate Identity audit team may need to go back to the raw data from previous surveys to analyse the different response from different sites or locations.

Questions on behavioral perceptions will include:

- What are the different parts of the organization like to deal with?

- Are representatives of the company polite or rude?

- How quickly are customers served or telephone calls answered and transferred?

- How helpful are staff in answering questions and resolving problems?

During Step 5 of the audit, which should take only about two months unless completely new research has to be undertaken, the audit team should meet regularly to compare notes.

SUMMARIZE
SALIENT POINTS

In most cases, a few salient points usually emerge quickly and clearly from the research. For example, during the course of a study for a major international pharmaceutical company operating under a variety of different names, it was clear that most outside audiences only knew the division of the company with which they were dealing. Most had no idea of the scope or size of the company, or even the country where it was based. They knew very little about its ownership and therefore underrated it in comparison with its competitors. What emerged most clearly during the internal interviews was that there was little respect for the center and no feeling of any common bond except the requirement to make more profits.

The audit of stationery, literature, environments and communications revealed that the group had no consistent way of describing its activities, had no standardized or commonly-used organization chart, had no standards for determining building styles, and communicated infrequently with its financial audiences, usually in times of crisis. The divisions shared no common visual themes and had no agreement as to where, when and how to support their own activities with the group name. Cheap, "over the counter" products often featured the group name in order to give them credibility, while sophisticated products developed with massive research and development efforts were promoted mainly through brand names.

In this case the "how are we perceived" issue was clear: as a mess. The "why we are perceived in this way" was also clear. Because the company presented itself in an incoherent and inconsistent fashion, it confused people both inside and outside its boundaries.

Why Are We Perceived in this Way?

In the example just given, the "how" and "why" are very closely related. This is not always the case. This assessment has already outlined a series of factors that combine to determine a company's identity. There are three basic types of identity previously discussed in this document (pages 6-7).

• Monolithic

• Endorsed

• Branded

Figure 12 shows three additional ways of subdividing these types, along with the benefits and constraints of each approach. In this case, the monolithic identity may be diluted (variations on a theme) or split (shared/dual). Midway between the endorsed identity and the branded identity lies the conditional identity. Analysis of these more-detailed options may help to provide a clearer picture of the company's existing status.

There are four components of an identity:

• product or service

• environment

• communication

• behavior

There are three means by which identity can be observed:

• visual symbols

• communication

• behavior

Finally, there are four disciplines through which an identity program is carried out:

Corporate Strategy. This includes the company's mission/vision, long-term and short-term business objectives. Ideally the corporate identity should be able to reflect and communicate what the company stands for.

Marketing. Corporate identity must support the company's marketing objectives, distinguish the company from the competition and position the company appropriately in the minds of its key publics.

Communication. All communications should clearly convey the corporate identity.

• When a company has a good image, the public is more likely to assume that it produces good products.

• The public is more likely to pay more for a company's products and buy their new products if the company has a good image.

• The public is more likely to take the company's side in disputes.

FIGURE 12
BRAND IDENTITY OPTIONS

BRAND IDENTITY OPTIONS	DESCRIPTION	BENEFITS	CONSTRAINTS
MONOLITHIC **MITSUBISHI**	One name, symbol, trade dress and typestyle for all products and divisions	• Cost-effective worldwide • Single focus reinforces brand identity • Simplifies new product/ company launch • Maximize advertising/ marketing dollars • Broad shareholder understanding • Builds strong brand equity	• More difficult to spin off products/divisions • Problems in one product/division can taint all • Strategy may require separation of certain products/divisions • May be politically unfeasible • Longer implementation
VARIATIONS ON A THEME Kodak / PRODUCTS BY Kodak	Variations of primary trade name, trade dress to provide differentiation of products while maintaining strong relationship to parent.	• Common theme elements unify and reinforce brand • Communicates diversity of products and services • Strong cross-sell potential • Cost-effective launch of new products/ services • Broader shareholder recognition	• More difficult to spin off products/divisions • Problems in one product/division can taint all • Strategy may require separation of certain products/divisions • May be politically unfeasible • Longer implementation
SHARED/DUAL **ITT Sheraton**	Links two strong brand identities. Linked brands may have primary/ secondary relationship or equal billing with parent/partner.	• Each identity may strengthen the other • Retains equity of both for leveraging potential • Facilitates uncomplicated brand spin-offs • Broader shareholder recognition • Shows relationship visually	• Synergy issues may constrain this approach • Problems in one product/division can taint all • Autonomous divisions/ brands may balk at this strategy causing political problems
ENDORSED AAFES	Parent provides umbrella under which individual brands are marketed.	• Leverages equity of parent throughout organization and with individual brands • Facilitates spin-offs with branded assets intact • Broader shareholder recognition • Strong cross-sell	• Can not spin off parent company's endorsement name or symbol with division/ product when brand is sold
CONDITIONAL *Campbell's* SWANSON	Existing, acquired or created brand/ divisional identities co-existing, sometimes with and sometimes without visual relationship to parent.	• Brands without strong link to parent can be spun off for profit • Return on investment may be reason for two separate strategies • Can sell competing products within same category	• Expensive way to support multiple brands on own merits, no synergy • The whole is less than the sum of its parts • Not easy to understand totality of company/ products
BRANDED AHp	Each product/division has its own individual identity.	• Brands can be bought and sold easily • Provides diversity and clear segment/niche market • Brands stand on own, not affected by problems in other categories • Can sell competing products within same category	• Most expensive method to manage brands • Minimal cross-sell, leveraging opportunities • Not easy to understand totality of company/ products • Brand equity must be built for each brand, no synergy • Who is the parent?

• The public is more likely to consider the company's stock a good investment, and the stock is likely to suffer less in a general market decline than will the stock of a company that does not have as good an image.

Organizational Behavior. The company can create and sustain a work environment that encourages employees to achieve the corporate mission and to project a positive image in all endeavors to further enhance the corporate identity.

By using this framework, the audit team can assess the critical factors that affect its identity and discover clues that will help them to know how the company is perceived. This should result in an analysis of how the current perception of the company compares with how leaders of the organization would like it to be seen. Then attention can be turned toward determining what factors make the difference between the actual identity being projected and the message the organization should communicate.

Why Is the Organization Misunderstood?

In many cases, the reasons why an organization is misunderstood are clear once the research has been completed. When it is not clear, however, the team should examine the identity of the organization through all of the tools outlined above in order to determine where there are anomalies, gaps, and contradictions that lead to misconceptions about the company's identity. What kind of identity does the company have: monolithic, thematic, dual, endorsed, conditional or decentralized/branded — or some combination of all these? If some parts of the organization are monolithic, others endorsed and still others branded, it may not be surprising that audiences are confused.

For example, a major international aerospace and defense company uses one single name for both its commercial aerospace group and its troubled defense business. A number of other names are used for the more rapidly-growing, technologically-sophisticated parts of its business. In other words, it has no clear identity structure. In addition, its newer technology-driven subsidiaries operate as relatively independent units which actively separate themselves from the group. This helps to explain why the parent company's size and scope are consistently underrated by people outside the company.

How does the mix of strategy, communication, marketing and organizational behavior affect the way the organization is perceived? That is illustrated by another example.

A conglomerate with a powerful, high-profile leader acquired a number of companies in a wide variety of industries. The companies were scattered geographically, and were acquired over a relatively short period of time. No one understood the company's structure, including the people who worked in it. Until recently, the company's leader made no attempt to explain his corporate policy or vision, and rarely explained why decisions were made. Consequently, his actions were often seen as being capricious.

To further confuse the issue, there were no consistent standards of product quality or type which tied the various divisions together. Businesses seemed to be bought and sold more or less at random. In reality, the leader's decisions were driven by an over-riding goal of exploiting what were seen to be under-exploited assets. Subsidiaries acquired or developed on this basis were then sometimes merged into larger, more variable units, or divested. All this was unexplained and was therefore incomprehensible to most people involved with the organization.

As the audit team does its work, it will come across examples of inconsistency in communications, in presentation, in behavior, and in strategy. When these inconsistencies are looked at as a whole, they usually explain why there are misconceptions about the size, scope and values of the organization under review.

Uncovering Issues

The process by which the audit team examines the "why" of how the company is perceived will sometimes uncover issues that are not, on the surface, directly associated with identity at all. For example, in a major industrial company whose identity was reviewed a few years ago, two teams from different divisions were developing essentially the same new product. This was because research and development efforts were not effectively co-ordinated from the center. The relationship between the center and the divisions was unclear on this and many similar issues, which led to waste and duplication of effort on a large scale. This lack of coordination was reflected not just in the identity structure, but in the performance and morale of the company as a whole.

A good identity audit will uncover issues familiar to some individuals within the organization, but that have not been considered in terms of their impact on the identity. It is likely that the early stages of the audit will have opened up other interesting and significant issues.

For example, there could be inconsistencies in presentation, waste and duplication in purchasing, sales and communication overlaps, and contradictions and missed opportunities in human resource management. In particular, the disciplines of corporate strategy, organizational behavior, communication and marketing — and the links (or lack of links) between them, and the reasons for this — will be exposed in this part of the audit.

DETERMINE THE OPTIONS FOR CHANGE

Determining the "how" and the "why" of establishing an appropriate identity will require ideas from beyond the audit team. The implications of what has been found should be examined by a broader group. Regardless of the results of the first two stages of the audit, the team must consider why the company is perceived as it is, and what should be done to change that perception if it is not in line with what the company wants to project.

This process leads to the question of visions. When an organization or parts of an organization are presented in an inconsistent, unclear, or contradictory fashion, the overall vision of the company needs to be more clearly articulated. In such cases, the vision has faded, was never clear in the first place, or has not taken into account changes within the company and its market place.

The duty of the audit team is to clarify the company's current identity and to press for a reconsideration of the company's vision. The vision should answer this question: What drives our business? Are we a business whose heart lies in technological excellence (such as Daimler-Benz), in understanding the consumer (as with Unilever), in developing new products and introducing them to market (like Glaxo), or do we have another priority? The company's vision will be further articulated in Step 9.

The audit team's role is to start a dialog on the subject of identity and the factors that contribute to the company's current identity. On a tactical level, the examples below will help to frame potential problems that the audit team may have uncovered and serve as tangible probes to help determine why the organization's corporate identity should change. Discussion of these examples and questions will help the audit team to focus on problems and opportunities faced by the organization as it reconsiders its identity.

Discussion examples for use in clarifying the company vision

- The company may be growing fast and furiously internally and through mergers and acquisitions. Each change is represented by a different look, so the composite shows a group of unrelated materials. Each time a change takes place, the top executives are presented with design decisions concerning names, trademarks, letterheads, and so on; and decisions have been made independently of previous decisions. Most outsiders and some insiders are therefore surprised when they are told about all the divisions of the company. They do not realize that it is so large and diversified; they cannot tell from the communication materials.

- If the collected communications materials vary depending upon which department or division they are from, the company probably looks disorganized to the outsider. A good image has a major impact on the public's opinion of the company's financial standing, its personnel, its products, and its reliability. Are key executives — notably the public relations director, the marketing, advertising, and sales managers, the purchasing agent, and the president — speaking the same language and to a common end? Are these executives communicating with each other?

- When viewed all together, does the visual output project a dynamic, organized company on the way up with solid foundations? Or does it make the company look like a gangling adolescent, all arms and legs, each going in a different direction? Does the company look like it is having a hard time trying to form a cohesive family organization that works as a team? Does it look like the executives have confidence in their positions on the team?

- Life is said to begin at forty. The company may be about to celebrate its fortieth year in business. Does it look its age? If so, the firm will not attract as many new, young employees as it could and should. It will find it difficult to relate to the "younger generation". With the buying power of this group, every company must relate to it. But until the company's sales stopped growing, managers did not seem to think they had to. Many established companies continue to grow (even if at a lesser rate with time) through sheer momentum. In the beginning, it is innovation, flexibility, and daring that cause success and growth. Once established, many companies lose this dynamism and with time are preempted by younger, innovative organizations. Do the visual materials look old, tired and inflexible?

- The corporation may have outstripped its one-store success-story long ago. In fact, it may also have outgrown its regional success story. It is now a national success. But success has not "spoiled" the company; it has not motivated it to change its image. It still looks the same as it did when it was a one-unit operation — as though one person is running the store, greeting the customers, and knows every employee. This image could be a plus but shouldn't the public also know how large the company is? Does the unchanged image meet all the different demands at prices it can afford? The building is the image. How can it be replaced, should it be replaced, and with what?

- The company's various divisions may be in different fields of retailing. They all do look alike and they do adhere to one graphic design system as depicted in the Graphic Manual for Corporate Identification, which has acted as the corporate Bible since the program's inception. However, is the graphic control system an exercise in rigidity? Is "status quo thinking" settling in over management? Is the firm promoting a look of corporate sterility or stagnation instead of corporate synergy and dynamism? Some corporations acquire other companies mainly for the top management of those companies. If the acquired entrepreneurs feel that their creativity or freedom is stifled within the framework of the identity program, there is danger that they will have been for nothing.

• In a group of companies, there are often reasons for continuing the separate images of the constituents. It takes great experience and design skill to create a system for a corporation that develops an organizational corporate discipline that is valuable in the financial world while allowing diversity. Do the communication materials gathered reflect this expertise?

• Finally, the audit team should ask whether the company can move into global markets with products and services in an economical way. Are the products and services dressed to travel and will they be welcome in other countries, or do they need a new trademark, trade name, and trade dress?

Step **8**

PRESENT THE
AUDIT RESULTS

The audit team should now present its analysis, along with the issues and implications that they see growing out of the identity audit, to the appropriate people for consideration. All of the points previously discussed — including the development of a new vision — are legitimate aspects of the work of the team. All have relevance to its findings and all are critical to improving corporate performance.

At this stage, the audit team should clearly understand the strategic options available to the organization in terms of corporate/brand identity. They should be trying to discover which strategic option each audience perceives as best for the organization. The team may wish to show to board members visual examples which demonstrate potential corporate identity options. The presentation of visual examples will help to focus the board's discussion of the audit results. If the board members are persuaded that the corporate identity is in need of attention and development, they may now seek the assistance of outside consultants to develop and implement a program.

The two examples illustrated below, Eastern Enterprises, a utility company, and Haworth, an international office furniture manufacturer, may be helpful.

Eastern Enterprises' identity system (shown in Figure 13) incorporates as many of the existing divisions' identities as possible, to provide continuity. The new symbol (bottom right) preserves the circle that was so prominent in many of their old company marks (top left); incorporated into it is an abstract impression of energy. The basic lettering style was built on the existing Boston Gas logo. The unifying mark and type style identify the various divisions as part of the total organization.

Haworth of Holland, Michigan, USA had acquired numerous office furniture manufacturers located in the United States, Europe and Asia. Its goal was to create a new corporate identity system which would build the value of the Haworth name internationally, while at the same time deriving the greatest possible benefit from the corporate image of the companies it had acquired.

FIGURE 14
A STUDY OF THE HAWORTH CORPORATE IDENTITY

ACQUIRED IDENTITIES

comforto

mueller

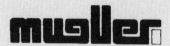

MODEL 1

comforto
A HAWORTH COMPANY

mueller
A HAWORTH COMPANY

MODEL 2

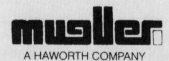

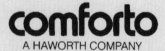

comforto
A HAWORTH COMPANY

mueller
A HAWORTH COMPANY

MODEL 3

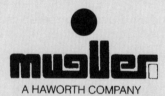

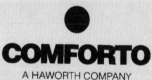

COMFORTO
A HAWORTH COMPANY

MUELLER
A HAWORTH COMPANY

MODEL 4

HAWORTH
COMFORTO PRODUCTS

HAWORTH
MUELLER PRODUCTS

MODEL 5

HAWORTH
OFFICE SYSTEMS

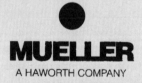

The first level of Figure 14 shows the logotypes of two of the companies acquired by Howarth. The remaining levels illustrate five corporate identity options (conceptual models) along a spectrum which begins with a decentralized, "branded" approach and moves all the way to a monolithic solution. The benefits of each approach are as follows:

Model 1

Established brand graphics are retained with the addition of a corporate endorsement. This alternative creates a relationship to Haworth while retaining the goodwill (equity) of the brand graphics.

Benefits:

- Haworth endorsement may strengthen the brand in some markets.

- Brand may strengthen Haworth in some markets.

- Facilitates spin-offs with brand assets intact.

- No loss of equity in brand graphics.

Constraints:

- Haworth endorsement may weaken the brand image in some markets.

- Haworth may look like manufacturer's representatives.

- Not easy to understand who Haworth is.

- Does not build Haworth corporate identity.

Model 2

As Model 1, with the addition of a unifying corporate symbol. This alternative develops a stronger relationship to Haworth while retaining equity.

Benefits:

- Equity in individual brands retained while building a stronger Haworth presence.

- Each identity would strengthen/cross-sell the other.

- Significant presence for Haworth in association with the individual brand equities.

• Individual brand equities show diversity and depth of Haworth product lines.

Constraints:

• Haworth symbol may not work well with existing brand graphics.

• Problems in one product/brand can taint all.

• Strategy may require separation or consolidation of certain products/brands.

Model 3

Retention of primary brand name to provide differentiation of products while projecting strong relationship to parent. This alternative provides a systematic identity, eliminating individual brand logotypes in favor of one style of graphic representation.

Benefits:

• Strong signal value of symbol builds Haworth brand equity faster.

• Common elements result in strong unification of brands.

• Communicates diversity of products.

• Strong cross-sell potential.

• Simplifies new product/company launch.

Constraints:

• Problems in one product/brand could possibly taint all.

• Risk loss of brand value by removal of an equity factor, if the brand graphics are well recognized.

Model 4

One name/symbol and typestyle for all products and divisions. This alternative makes a strong, consistent Haworth presentation. Haworth is the dominant identity in brand communications; the brands are secondary.

Benefits:

• Cost-effective worldwide.

- Single focus reinforces corporate identity.

- Simplifies new product/company launch.

- Maximizes advertising/marketing spend.

- Builds strong, singular brand equity.

Constraints:

- More difficult to spin off products/brands.

- Problems in one product/brand could possibly taint all.

- Risk loss of brand value by removal of an equity factor, if the brand graphics are well recognized.

Model 5

The individual brands are submerged in this monolithic alternative. Haworth is the only identity.

Benefits:

- Cost-effective worldwide.

- Single focus reinforces corporate identity.

- Simplifies new product/company launch.

- Maximizes advertising/marketing spend.

- Builds strong, singular brand equity.

Constraints:

- More difficult to spin off products/brands as assets.

- Risk loss of brand value by removal of an equity factor, if the brand graphics are well recognized.

USE THE AUDIT DATA
TO IMPROVE THE
CORPORATE IDENTITY

In most cases, the implementation of an identity program will require the help of outside consultants. Few executives have had experience with developing corporate identity programs. Therefore, it is often appropriate to set up an internal system with the built-in support of key people who support the development of a corporate identity program and have the influence to implement it. The members of the internal audit team could be given the responsibility of finding an appropriate consultancy and sharing the audit information with the outside consultants. The outside consultants would augment the contribution of the internal team because of their experience, objectivity, and expertise. The internal audit team could form the core of the larger steering group working with the consultancy.

Setting Up the Identity Structure

Developing a corporate identity is a specialized business. The identity program embraces business disciplines that range widely across the corporation. It influences both the internal and external audiences of the corporation. It is therefore essential that the identity program be set up carefully. An effective corporate identity program is managed at both the top and the middle levels of the organization. There must be commitment to the program from the board and the CEO. The program is spearheaded/led by a senior executive from marketing or corporate communications, who will be given the appropriate authority and access to resources, and work directly with the CEO on the program. It is often helpful if the executive in charge of the program has a marketing or communications background.

Establishing the Working Party

Once a decision has been made about whether or not to use outside consultants, and any consultants have been appointed, a small working party should be formed consisting of people both from the consultancy and from the client organization. It is vital that the working party represent those parts of the company that will be most affected by the program. In particular, there should be representation from corporate strategy, marketing, communications and organizational behavior. It is sometimes useful if purchasing, legal and technical people are also available to lend their expertise. With the CEO, the working party should attempt to determine the scope of the corporate identity program. Sometimes it may be useful if the working party reports to a small, senior-level steering committee.

Not all identity programs are comprehensive. Some deal with the whole corporation, others with part of the company, and some deal only with the company's brands.

Some involve only the visual and structural aspects of identity. Whether the program has a broad or relatively narrow objective, however, it should follow some version of the methodology outlined below. This outline is appropriate for a large-scale corporate identity program.

Developing and Articulating the Vision

At this point in the program, the issue of vision must be fully addressed. The vision must be based both upon the reality of the organization and on what it believes it can realistically become. Each company is unique: each has unique strengths than can be clearly articulated. No company should attempt to copy its competitors, so each corporate vision will be unique. The corporate vision is arrived at after assessing the reality of the company's strengths and weaknesses, after studying how it is perceived by its various audiences, and after examining its potential for development. The vision has to be projected in a form that all audiences of the organization can see and understand intuitively and immediately.

Just as the existing corporate identity was measured in terms of written and oral communication, behavior and visual presentation, so the vision will be communicated in these same ways. While there is a trend toward giving equal emphasis to all three of these channels, visual identity, or the way the corporation looks, remains the most potent weapon in symbolizing change and communicating a vision, both to internal and external audiences.

At the heart of the visual identity is the nomenclature and identification system, and the way it is reflected in symbols and logotypes. The symbol is highly visible. Its prime purpose is to present the vision of the corporation with impact, brevity and immediacy. It should encapsulate the entire identity idea. Because of this, it often becomes the focal point from which the whole identity is subsequently judged.

It is not always desirable to change the symbol when a new corporate identity program is launched. In some cases, modification of the symbol may be more appropriate. Organizations that have spent millions on promoting their existing symbols over a period of years are more likely to wish to modify what they have, rather than change it completely. The illustration in Figure 15 shows a logotype which was modified to reflect a changing corporate vision.

FIGURE 15
MODIFICATIONS OF ICI LOGO

However, there are also situations when it is desirable to make a clean break and produce a new visual symbol. This usually happens because the old symbol no longer communicates the company's vision clearly.

In some cases, the name of the company or its products may even be changed. The case of Forte (illustrated in Figure 16) shows how a change in visual symbol supported a larger change in vision. Each case must be examined individually in order to determine the level of change that is appropriate.

FIGURE 16
FROM THF TO FORTE

The decision to change a name and symbol must not be taken lightly; neither should it be dismissed as an option simply because of the expense and difficulty involved in changing. Some of the issues that will affect the decision include the nature of the business that the company is in, its reputation within the industry, its plans for growth and development, and the extent to which perceptions of the organization are in line with realities or with the vision the company hopes to project. If leaders of an organization decide to change the company's symbol, a new visual identity should be developed in conjunction with consultants or professionals involved in the project. They should produce a series of possible visual approaches applied to a range of corporate activities. Eventually, one of these approaches will be chosen and developed so that it can be integrated into the visible manifestations of the company and its brands.

Identity Program Launch and Introduction

If the new corporate identity program is to be implemented successfully, it has to be launched with enthusiasm and commitment. The launch is the first major opportunity for the corporation's leaders to present the identity as a significant corporate resource and to integrate it into the organizational structure. The launch of an identity program takes place in two phases: 1) internal and 2) external. People inside the company must be committed to, and informed about, the new identity before it emerges publicly, so it is essential that the internal launch of an identity program take place before the external launch. The internal launch normally takes the form of seminars, discussions and audiovisual presentations. At these activities the corporate vision on which the identity is based must be explained clearly and simply. The place of the vision as part of the company's philosophy must be demonstrated. The commitment of management to drive home the vision through communication and behavior as well as through the new visual program must be emphasized. At the internal launch, it is essential to explain that this visual part of the identity is simply the means by which the corporate vision is communicated.

The external launch will involve advertising, brochures, sales meetings, and a press relations drive. It will have a somewhat different emphasis from the internal launch, although the fundamental message will be the same. It is worth remembering that external audiences are not as interested in, or concerned about, the company as the internal audience is. Outsiders are also likely to be more skeptical, so it is essential to avoid extravagant claims or windy verbiage.

Where the company has a dealer organization, the external launch should be divided into two stages: first, the dealer and special customer launch, and second, a public launch.

Program Implementation: Cost and Time Schedules

A cost, time and method schedule for the launch and subsequent implementation of the program must be prepared at the same time as detailed design work is taking place. The following factors have to be taken into account:

• Who will be responsible for running the program inside the company?

It is essential that this job be held by an executive with influence, tact, and preferably, experience. He or she will be responsible directly to the chief executive and should be called the Identity Manager.

• At what speed is the implementation program going to be managed? There are four choices here:

— An overnight change from old to new.

— A controlled change taking place very quickly, over a period of about one year.

— A controlled but more gradual change, over 3-5 years.

— Gradual replacement on an ad hoc basis.

The method chosen depends upon how drastic the identity change is. The more dramatic the change, the more rapidly the new identity should be introduced. Other factors to be taken into consideration include the current economic climate, marketing and internal issues.

ONGOING MANAGEMENT OF THE IDENTITY PROGRAM

Other aspects of the corporate environment should be taken into consideration in rolling out the corporate identity program. One of the most important of these is ensuring that the program has adequate funding and is supported by adequate authority. Some of the variables to be taken into account are outlined below:

- Who is going to pay for the program: the center or the operating units?

- How should liaison between the company's different subsidiaries and geographic divisions and the central identity resource work?

- How should the resource be staffed and how many people should it have?

- Where should it be located?

- What are the lines of responsibility?

- How should the roles of the different disciplines (strategy, marketing, communication and organizational behavior) be co-ordinated?

There is always a danger that after the excitement of the investigation, design and launch work, continuing attention to the identity program will be neglected. Implementation is essentially a long-term process. It requires getting people inside the organization to develop a clear instinct, intuition or feel for what is and what is not appropriate in terms of projecting the organization's image. At one level it involves substance (stationery, signs, packaging, replacing one set of colors and one logotype with another). From this standpoint, a control manual providing forms of the logotype for a variety of uses is becoming the norm. This can be made available on computer with software readily accessible to every part of the organization involved in public communications.

At a more basic and significant level, however, the corporate identity involves emotion, or the creation of a situation where people both inside and outside the company develop a feel for what is appropriate. The identity program cannot rely completely on the availability of a control manual. The management of the organization must create and sustain a sense of commitment to the newly-established identity and the agreed-upon corporate vision. The role of the board and more particularly the CEO in emphasizing the significance of the vision for maintaining long term corporate competitiveness is key.

As the company changes, acquires new subsidiaries, moves into new activities and develops new products, the corporate identity must be used appropriately and modified when necessary. The identity must adapt to new situations as they develop.

What to Expect Once the Program Is in Place

The corporate identity program will have an impact on brands, branding and product design, on the design and maintenance of buildings, on advertising campaigns, on personnel policies and recruitment, management and training, on purchasing practices, and on a wide variety of other corporate activities. Essentially, running a program effectively depends on achieving the appropriate balance between the requirements of different departments and divisions in a variety of geographic areas. The logistics of the program should also take into account the changing priorities and requirements of the corporation as a whole. From time to time there will be a conflict of interest or opinion between the functional divisions and departments and the Identity Manager. Where the dispute cannot be resolved at an appropriate level, it should go for arbitration. The working party, or another appropriate group, should meet regularly (perhaps every two months) to review progress on the identity and to arbitrate when necessary between the differing interests within the organization.

SUGGESTIONS FOR A SMALL-SCALE IDENTITY PROGRAM

While a major corporate identity program will be concerned with all aspects of the company's being and take into account all its subsidiaries and brands, it is not always possible or necessary to carry out such a comprehensive program. Sometimes a group of brands, or one or more divisions of a larger organization, will be the subject of an identity program. There is nothing wrong with carrying out an identity program for part of an operation, provided that its impact on the whole is understood. Here are some of the issues with which a more limited corporate program may be concerned for a group of brands or subsidiary companies.

Name or Names

• Do we have too many different names?

• Do we need a new name?

• How can we relate brand names or names to the corporate name? Do we have a monolithic, branded or endorsed identity?

Visual Identity

• Should we strengthen the existing identity?

• Should we create an entirely new visual identity?

• How, if at all, do we relate the identity of the part with which we are dealing with the whole?

BENEFITS OF
A CORPORATE
IDENTITY
PROGRAM

A corporate identity program must be seen as part of the process by which the corporation explains and differentiates itself. It is a vehicle by which the corporation's vision of itself can be perceived and understood. Specifically, a clear corporate identity brings the following benefits to the company:

- It enables the organization to tell the people with whom they deal what they stand for, what they are, what they do and how they do it. It enables representatives of the company to explain how their activities relate to each other.

- It encourages tighter and more coherent messages of all types to emerge from the corporation.

- It enables people who deal with the company to understand its goals and objectives.

These advantages result in other benefits when a corporate identity program is well-organized:

Internal Benefits

- Morale and motivation improve.

- Employee turnover drops.

- Product quality improves.

- The company has an advantage in recruiting talented people.

- People within the organization work together more effectively.

Financial Benefits

- The company's qualities are recognized in financial circles, thus encouraging the price of the stock to rise.

- Acquisitions are made more easily.

- Organizations are better protected against predators.

Marketing Benefits

• Consumers are more likely to look favorably upon the company and its products and to be brand loyal.

• Suppliers operate more consistently.

• Expenditures are more cost-effective in terms of activities and promotion.

• The company can establish itself more effectively in new markets.

• New activities can emerge more rapidly within a company.

WHAT WILL IT ALL COST AND HOW LONG WILL IT TAKE?

A corporate identity program is normally excellent value for what it costs. It allows the company to develop a consistent, meaningful, co-ordinated and permanent image throughout all its activities for little more than the price of an advertising campaign. The cost depends largely on timing. When an organization is launching a new name and visual identity, it has to make a major impact, so it will have to move fast and the costs will be higher. When, as is often the case, the existing identity is modified, the introduction can be lower key with the program of implementation more gradual. Therefore, the costs can be lower and spread out over a longer period. Apart from the origination work, corporate identity costs are usually dealt with as part of annual departmental budgets. Money is already allocated for signs to be repainted, stationery to be reprinted, vehicles to be replaced, etc. Costs can generally be divided into the following categories:

- Consultant fees.

- Cost for creating new materials (such as advertising, videos, new behavioral policies).

- Cost for launching the identity (advertising, videos etc.).

- Replacement costs—those costs involved in replacing existing materials which would have needed replacing anyway (stationery, vehicle liveries, etc.).

- Costs for instituting new systems in personnel, purchasing and so on (these may be difficult to calculate).

The cost of each program should be projected in stages. A fixed budget for time and costs should be established for the initial stages. Variations should be allowed if the program changes. There should be a clear separation between fees and costs of manufacture. Subsequent costs should be worked out as the project develops and its total approximate size can be estimated. Particularly during implementation, costs should be individually negotiated for separate projects.

SUMMARY

As corporations become more complex, as their products become more similar, as the inter-relationship between organizations becomes more intricate, corporate identity becomes mandatory as a corporate resource that tells people the who, the what, the why and the whither of a company's existence. Like other management systems that operate continuously in organizations, a corporate identity process should be developed which allows for the regular re-evaluation of perceptions of the organization by its important audiences, and for the re-formulation or re-establishment of the company's vision when it has been forgotten or become outdated. This will contribute to the organization's ability to remain competitive in a world that is becoming ever more complex.

Part 2

THE AUDIT PROCESS

This section addresses the logistical and process requirements of conducting an audit. The topics covered in this section include:

• Staffing the audit team

• Creating an audit project plan

• Laying the groundwork for the audit

• Analyzing audit results

• Sharing audit results

• Writing effective audit reports

• Dealing with resistance to audit recommendations

• Building an ongoing audit program

STAFFING THE AUDIT TEAM

Who conducts the audit is as important in many ways as how the audit is conducted. In fact, the people selected for the audit team will, in large part, determine how the audit is done, how results are analyzed, and how findings are reported. The following list includes general characteristics of effective audit teams for most areas:

- Consists of three to four people.

- Reports to CEO or other senior executive.

- Represents a carefully selected range of skills and experience.

More than four people may be needed for an audit team if data gathering is labor intensive, as when large numbers of customers or employees must be interviewed. However, audit teams of more than six or seven people present problems of maintaining uniformity and communicating audit progress and findings during the course of the evaluation.

Selecting an Audit Team Leader

The audit team leader will play a strong role in shaping both the data gathering and the findings from the audit. The strength of the team leader will also influence the acceptance of the audit, both in terms of enlisting cooperation in the data gathering phase and in securing support for improvement initiatives that grow out of the audit. Because of the importance of this role, care should be taken in selecting the appropriate person for the job. The following qualities are found in successful audit team leaders:

- Has a good relationship with the CEO or with the executive-level sponsor of the audit.

- Is well-liked and well-respected at all levels of the organization, especially in the area to be audited.

- Has good interpersonal skills; can maintain good relationships even in difficult circumstances.

- Has good analytical skills; can assimilate and process large amounts of complex data quickly.

71

• Has some knowledge of the function or area being audited.

• Has extensive knowledge of the type of process being audited.

• Communicates ideas clearly and effectively.

Skills to Be Represented on the Audit Team

Once the team leader has been chosen, audit team members should be selected on the basis of what each can bring to the project. Selection efforts should focus on developing a balanced representation of the following qualities:

• A variety of tenures in the organization, with relative newcomers preferably having experience in other organizations.

• A variety of familiarity with the area (function or site) being audited. Those who are intimately familiar with the area can serve as guides to the less familiar; those who are new to the area can provide objectivity and ask questions that might never be considered by those more involved in the area.

• Considerable familiarity with the type of process being audited. For this reason, many organizations call on people filling roles in similar processes from other parts of the company to work on audit teams.

• Good analytical skills.

• Good interpersonal skills.

• Good facilitation and interviewing skills.

• Good communication skills.

• An understanding of the company's strategy and direction.

CREATING AN AUDIT PROJECT PLAN

Creating an audit project plan accomplishes the following objectives:

- Ensures the allocation of adequate resources, or helps audit team members be prepared to improvise in the face of short resources.

- Ensures the audit is timed so resources are available that may be in high demand.

- Creates clear expectations in the minds of team members about what must be done, and when — especially important when they are not committed to the project full-time.

- Ensures accountability for what must be done, who is responsible for which tasks, and when the audit must be completed.

Financial audits often rely on the Critical Path Method (CPM) of project planning. This method was originally developed by the US Department of Defense during World War II to facilitate the timely completion of weapons development and production. It has since been modified to plan a wide variety of projects. The following outline is a simplification of CPM. It suggests the aspects of a project that should be taken into account during the planning phase.

Critical Path Method

In developing the project plan, audit team members should ask and answer the following questions:

- *What tasks must be performed?*

This list should include the major tasks outlined in the audits, along with subtasks that grow out of those major headings. It should also include any tasks mandated by unique circumstances in the company performing the self-assessment. The audit team may want to brainstorm about tasks that need to be performed, then refine the list to reflect the work priorities of the audit.

• *In what order will the tasks be completed?*

Answering this question should include an analysis of which tasks and sub tasks are dependent on others. Which tasks cannot begin until another has been completed? Which tasks can be done at any time? The audit team may want to place the ordered task on a time line, with start dates, expected duration of the step, and end dates outlined for each task.

• *Who will perform each task?*

Most tasks will be performed by members of the audit team. These assignments should be made by taking the strengths of each team member into consideration, as well as the time availability of each person. Equity of work load should also be taken into account. If tasks are to be assigned to people not on the audit team, those individuals should be included or consulted at this point.

• *What resources will be needed for each step?*

Each task should be analyzed in terms of the personnel, budget, equipment, facilities, support services, and any other resources that will be needed for its completion. The team should assess the availability of all of the resources. Consideration should be given to the task ordering completed earlier. Are some resources subject to competing demands, and therefore difficult to secure at a particular time? How far in advance do arrangements for resources need to be made? Does the task order or time line need to be revised in light of what is known about resource availability?

• *Where is the slack time?*

Slack time is unscheduled time between dependent tasks. Slack provides a degree of flexibility in altering the start dates of subsequent tasks. Slack time signals that a task has a range of possible start dates. It is used to determine the critical path.

• *What is the critical path?*

The critical path in a project is the set of tasks that must be completed in a sequential, chronological order. If any task on the critical path is not completed, all subsequent tasks will be delayed. Delays at any point in the critical path will result in an equivalent delay in the completion of the total project.

Regardless of the method used to develop the project plan, no project, regardless how simple, is ever completed in exact accordance with its plan. However, having a project plan allows the team to gauge its progress, anticipate problems and determine where alternative approaches are needed.

LAYING THE GROUNDWORK FOR THE AUDIT

Once the team has been selected and a project plan developed, the audit leader should prepare those who will be involved in and affected by the audit for the team's visit or for data-gathering. The following steps will help the audit to run more smoothly:

Communicate Executive Support for the Audit

Demonstrating executive support for the audit accomplishes two goals. First, it increases the chances that those involved in the area being audited will cooperate with data gathering efforts. Second, it shows executive support for the area being audited and suggests a commitment to improving the area's performance.

In many companies, the audit is introduced by the executive sponsor of the audit by means of a memo. The memo should explain the purpose of the audit and ask for the support of everyone in the area being audited. This memo is distributed to everyone within the company who will be affected by or involved in the data gathering process. The most effective memos explain how the audit results will be used, reassuring those who will be responding to audit team requests about the motives of the audit. The credibility of such memos is also bolstered when previous audits have been acted upon with positive results.

Make Arrangements with the Area to Be Audited

The audit team leader should check with the appropriate manager in charge of the process or site being audited to arrange for any required on-site visits, interviewing, surveys, focus groups, or written information needed for the audit. The team leader should also explain the purpose, scope, and expected duration of the audit; review the project plan with the manager; and answer any questions the manager has about the audit.

The team leader should also work with the appropriate manager or managers to determine how the audit can be conducted with the least impact on the flow of work. This may include discussions about the timing of the audit, the options for data gathering, the availability of needed data, and possibilities for generating the necessary information quickly and easily. Finding ways to make data collection more efficient and effective is especially important when the audit is part of an ongoing program, rather than an isolated assessment.

Develop a Protocol or Checklist

A protocol or checklist can be used by the audit team to outline the issues that are central to the audit. Written guides can help the leaders of those areas being audited to prepare for the audit. A protocol represents a plan of what the audit team will do to accomplish the objectives of the audit. It is an important tool of the audit, since it not only serves as the audit team's guide to collecting data, but also as a record of the audit procedures completed by the team. In some cases, audit teams may even want to format the checklist in a way that allows them to record their field notes directly on the checklist.

The checklist should include no more than twenty major items, and checklists should be updated with each audit in order to ensure that the appropriate measures are taken. Items where improvement initiatives have been successful should be eliminated from the checklist, with newly identified possibilities for improvement opportunities added.

Analyzing
Audit Results

Discovering gaps between a company's targets and its actual performance is a relatively easy task. Tools are provided to assist audit teams in assessing their performance in a given area. In most cases, more opportunities for improvement will be uncovered by an audit than can be addressed by the resources and energy available. Therefore, one of the most difficult aspects of analyzing the results of an audit lies in determining which opportunities are the most important for managers to pursue.

Because resources and energy for pursuing improvement initiatives are limited, choices must be made about which options are most important. Sometimes these decisions are based on political winds in the company, or on what has worked well in the past, or on personal preferences of top management. However, scarce resources will be used more effectively if allocated to the areas where they will have the greatest impact. Managers must also determine the most effective way to approach initiatives. This section discusses criteria for prioritizing opportunities that grow out of audit findings.

The Novations Strategic Alignment Model

The mid-1980s saw the birth of the "excellence" movement, where many companies tried to achieve excellence in every area of endeavor. Although the movement created an awareness of the need for management improvements, it failed to consider that not all management processes are equal in terms of producing benefits. As a result, leading organizations in today's environment focus on performing well in a few core areas. Knowing what those core areas are depends on a clear vision of the company's strategy.

Strategic thinking about which areas should be improved involves much more than taking an inventory of current capabilities and weaknesses. If it did not, existing capabilities would always determine strategic objectives, and organizational growth and development would come to a halt. To set priorities strategically, companies must decide which improvement opportunities fall in the following categories:

• What to do themselves.

• What to do with someone else.

• What to contract others to do.

• What not to do.

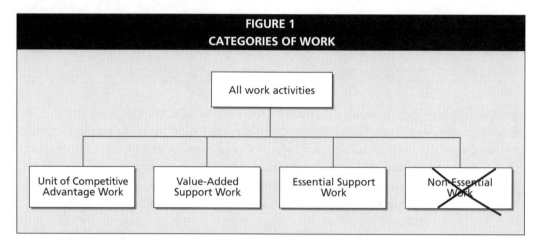

Figure 1 illustrates the four categories of work.

Unit of Competitive Advantage (UCA) Work includes work and capabilities that create distinctiveness for the business in the marketplace.

Value-added Support Work facilitates the accomplishment of the UCA work. For example, a company may have a technology orientation rather than a service orientation, but an effective logistics process may help them to improve their UCA work of providing cutting edge technology.

Essential Support Work neither creates advantage nor facilitates the work that creates advantage, but must be done if businesses are to continue to operate (includes such things as paying taxes, maintaining payroll records, etc.).

Nonessential Work is activity that has lost its usefulness but continues to be done because of tradition.

Despite their sophistication in dealing with other aspects of business, most managers have archaic views of the different types of work. Many of their models for characterizing work have come from a finance or accounting orientation. Accounting terms such as overhead, direct labor, and indirect labor may be useful as a way to report costs, but they provide little understanding about the relative strategic importance of the work. Yet these classifications are frequently used to determine how work is organized and where resources are allocated.

The concept of *unit of competitive advantage* (UCA) helps to explain why some organizations either emphasize the wrong capabilities or de-emphasize the right capabilities. UCA also explains why some forms of improvement lead to competitive disadvantage, and why some businesses consistently outperform their competitors by gaining greater leverage from their competitive advantages.

A company's UCA includes the critical processes that create distinctiveness within an established strategic direction. It is based on the premise that businesses create competitive advantage when they focus their attention on a few key processes and implement those key processes in world-class fashion. For example, continuous improvement is a popular management program that assumes benefit from any kind of ongoing improvement. Generally speaking, however, continuous improvement programs will only create competitive advantage when an organization defines a strategic direction, clarifies strategic objectives, and determines its UCA. These crucial prerequisites tell where continuous improvement efforts should be focused to create maximum leverage. They suggest what kinds of work to improve interdependently, what kinds to improve separately, and what kinds not to waste time on. They even signal when continuous improvement is more likely to create competitive disadvantage rather than competitive advantage.

UCA Initiatives Should Take Priority

Understanding what work falls under which categories requires a clear understanding of the company's strategy. The initiatives resulting from an audit that affect the Unit of Competitive Advantage work processes should clearly have the highest priority among improvement projects. Value-added support initiatives should be second priority, and essential support work should be the third priority. Nonessential work should not be continued.

Once improvement opportunities that will have the greatest impact on the achievement of the company's goals have been identified, the following ideas can be used to lend further insight into how opportunities identified through an audit should be prioritized:

• *Focus on the two or three most important areas.*

Insisting that action be taken on all of the problems uncovered by the audit may overwhelm the people who are responsible for bringing about those changes. Flatter organizations and leaner work forces mean that people are already being asked to do more work with fewer resources and less time. Producing a long list of improvement initiatives may prompt people to dismiss all of them because they don't have time to complete the whole list.

• *Focus on the areas that can be changed.*

Emphasizing problems that are beyond the control of the people who are responsible to work on process improvement only leads to cynicism and a sense of powerlessness. By focusing on things that are within the sphere of influence, accountability for each part of the action plan can be clearly defined.

• *Include as priorities some improvements that can be made quickly.*

Rapid, visible improvement helps build support for more complicated initiatives. Quick improvements also reassure people of management's support for long-term improvement. Seeing immediate improvement helps to build commitment at all levels to the process, and helps build momentum for further change.

• *Emphasize the improvements that seem essential to long-term success.*

Essential improvements may involve sensitive issues or difficult problems, such as deficiencies in fundamental skill levels within the organization or basic strategy issues. These problems are not only difficult and expensive to address, but may also cause a great deal of personal pain or require significant individual adjustment. Nevertheless, long-term improvement requires a commitment to dealing with difficult issues rather than avoiding them.

SHARING AUDIT RESULTS

In most cases, audit results will be presented to various interested people in a feedback meeting. Those in attendance may include members of the executive team, managers who work in the area covered by the audit, the audit team members, and anyone else who is affected by or interested in the results. The meeting should be conducted by members of the audit team. The purpose is to present their findings, and make recommendations for capitalizing on opportunities for improvement.

Conducting Effective Feedback Meetings

The audit team's strategy for the meeting should be to present a clear and simple picture of the current situation as revealed by the audit. This may be a moment of truth for those who have been anticipating the audit results. The feedback meeting for an audit holds both excitement and anxiety: excitement that the future will be bright, and anxiety that shortcomings in individual performance will be highlighted and demands made for personal change. As a result, the meeting must be carefully managed in order to lead to productive change. The following structure is one recommended format for conducting a feedback meeting.

• *Introduce the meeting and preview its agenda.*

This might include an overview of the original intent of the audit, introduction of the audit team, and a brief summary of the meeting's agenda. This step should take no more than five minutes.

• *Present the audit findings.*

Audit findings should summarize the most important points revealed by the data gathered in the audit process. They should be presented separately from the audit recommendations in order to allow people to digest the two parts of the presentation separately. Clearing up misunderstandings about the findings may make the group more accepting of the team's recommendations.

The presentation of the audit findings should take comparatively little time. Audits almost always generate much more data than can be effectively presented or digested in a feedback meeting. The goal of the audit team should be to zero in on the two or three most important points learned from the audit, and present enough supporting data to illustrate those points.

Presenting too much data about audit findings has a number of negative effects. It encourages people to conduct their own analysis of the audit data. To a certain extent, this is a healthy and normal reaction. If others understand the evidence that supports the conclusions drawn by the audit team, they are more likely to accept and own the audit results. Therefore, they will be more committed to the changes brought about by the audit results. However, when people immerse themselves in large amounts of data, they may become victims of "analysis paralysis": they may spend unnecessary time attempting to explain contradictory data, or trying to understand methods used by others to gather data.

• *Present audit recommendations.*

Presenting the audit recommendations should be the central point of the meeting. The recommendations should grow out of the data highlights presented. The audit team should view the recommendations as discussion points for the meeting, rather than as absolute action items.

A common mistake in feedback meetings is to spend most of the meeting on presenting data and recommendations. It is easy for audit team members to become enamored of data they have invested considerable time and energy to collect and analyze. Others in the audience will probably also be interested in the details of the data collected. However, if too much time is spent on discussing the recommendations, the meeting will end before a commitment to action has been made.

• *Ask others to react to the data.*

The reactions of top management and those responsible for implementing audit recommendations will determine the ultimate value of the audit data. Therefore, the feedback meeting is a good time to resolve questions or problems with the findings and recommendations as they have been presented. If resistance to the audit findings is not resolved in the feedback meeting, opportunities for improvement may be lost.

Those attending the meeting may offer their opinions willingly. If not, the audit team members should ask the others in the room for their reaction to what has been presented.

• *Develop preliminary action plans.*

The detailed action plans should grow out of the recommendations made by the audit team. They should specifically address the question of who should do what by when. Formal accountability mechanisms should be established before the end of the meeting, such as the scheduling of subsequent meetings or follow-up check points.

WRITING EFFECTIVE AUDIT REPORTS

There are three fundamental purposes for writing a formal report at the conclusion of an audit:

- An audit report may be a stand-alone summary of the audit. This approach is not recommended, inasmuch as the report is likely to be filed away, making the probability of action unlikely.

- The report may supplement a feedback meeting, providing those in attendance with documentation and an outline to follow.

- The report should also serve as a baseline document to make measurement of performance improvement possible in future audits.

Because the written report is the most enduring part of the audit presentation, it should be well written and easy to understand. The following tips will lead to the preparation of effective written audit reports.

Focus on a Few Key Points

The audit presentation should focus on the two or three most important findings. It is impossible to present all of the data gathered in the audit to those who were not on the audit team. It is also not advisable to present every detail of the data. The audit team members should trust their own judgment about what the highlights of the study were, and present enough data to support that judgment. For each of the major findings, the team may want to include the following information:

- What is the problem?

- Why does it exist?

- What happens if the problem is not fixed:
  — in the short term?
  — in the long term?

- Recommend solutions.

- Outline expected benefits.

Prepare an Outline Before Writing the First Draft

A good outline ensures that the logic of the report is clear, and that ideas proceed in an order that makes sense. The following outline provides one approach that works effectively.

Background

This section should establish the framework for the audit in terms of:

• Providing a brief discussion of the overall purpose of the audit.

• Identifying the role of the audit team in the overall process.

• Establishing the limitations of the audit methodology to ensure that others utilize the results provided in the report appropriately.

Objectives

This section should identify specific objectives of the audit in terms of types of information the team was expected to generate.

Methodology

The methodology section should describe the mechanics of the audit and include the following information:

• Types of assessment used (survey, interviews, focus groups, etc.).

• Data sources, or the sample groups for each of the types of assessment used.

• Time frame during which the audit was conducted.

• Other pertinent details about how the audit was conducted.

Findings

This section is designed to provide others with a review of the "facts" that came out of the audit. Except in cases where an audit checks regulatory compliance, only the most significant findings should be discussed in any detail in the report. This section should also include briefly presented data supporting the findings.

Conclusions

This section should report the audit team's interpretation of what the facts of the audit mean in light of the objectives stated at the outset of the audit.

Recommendations

This section includes suggestions from the audit team on how to close the performance gaps identified in the audit. The degree of specificity to be included in the audit report will vary from company to company and audit to audit.

Appendix

This portion of the formal report should include any of the following items that are relevant to the audit:

• A copy of any questionnaires or survey instruments used in the audit.

• A summary of the data gathered in the course of the audit.

• Recommendations for subsequent audits based on the team's experience.

Present Audit Findings Accurately

Those who read the report will no doubt be somewhat familiar with the area covered by the audit. They may notice discrepancies between what they know about the subject and what is reported in the written document. Spotting one inaccuracy may lead the readers to discredit all of the findings, conclusions and recommendations. Audit team members should be careful to report data as it was actually generated, and to describe the impact of the findings accurately.

Use Clear, Concise Language

Every statement included in the report should be based on sound evidence developed or reviewed during the audit. Whatever is said must be supported or supportable. Speculation should be avoided. Generalities and vague reporting will only confuse and mislead those that the report should influence or inform. For example, a report using the terms *some*, *a few*, or *not all* can leave the reader confused about the significance of the finding. Specific quantities should be used, such as, "of the ten samples taken, two were found to be…", "Three of five respondents said that…", and so on. Statements should be qualified as needed, and any unconfirmed data or information should be identified as such.

Ideas or sentences that do not amplify the central theme should be eliminated. The report should not identify individuals or highlight the mistakes of individuals.

Use Good Grammar and Style

Basic grammar and style rules should be followed in writing the text. Below are some examples:

- Avoid extreme terms, such as alarming, deplorable, gross negligence, etc.

- Avoid using redundant or lengthy phrases, such as calling something an emergency situation when the word emergency alone will do.

- Avoid verbs camouflaged as nouns or adjectives. For example, use "the new procedure will reduce error entries," rather than "The new procedure will accomplish a reduction of error entries."

- Avoid indirect expressions where possible. For example, "Many instances of poor management were found," is more direct than saying, "There were many instances of poor judgment found."

- Use short, familiar words. Use words that are easily understandable to everyone and that convey the message concisely.

- Keep sentences short. Most writing experts suggest that an average sentence should be between 15 and 18 words. Packing too many ideas into a single sentence confuses and tires readers.

The audit team should provide enough background information in the report so that the reader clearly understands who conducted the audit and what the audit did or did not include. The purpose of the report as well as the purpose and scope of the audit should also be described in a manner that enables the reader to know why the report was written and who should take corrective action.

Timing of the Report

The timing of audit reports is critical to the overall reporting process and must be carefully thought out. In many cases, a written draft of the audit report is prepared one to three weeks before the feedback meeting. This draft then goes through a review and another report is prepared in time for the team's presentation. A final report may be completed after the feedback session has been held in order to record changes resulting from that meeting.

DEALING WITH RESISTANCE TO RECOMMENDATIONS

Most audit teams feel that if they can present their ideas clearly and logically, and have the best interests of the company or department at heart, managers will accept the recommendations made as part of the audit and follow the team's recommendations. Many people who have worked in organizations, however, find that no matter how reasonably recommendations are presented, they are all too often not implemented.

Implementation usually fails because it requires people to change their ways of working. That change requires a great deal of effort, energy, and risk; therefore, change is usually resisted. Resistance is an emotional process; people may embrace recommendations based on their logic, but fail to implement them because of the emotional resistance to the personal change involved. Resistance is a predictable, natural, and necessary part of the learning process. Although resistance may cause audit team members to feel they have missed the mark in terms of the recommendations they have made, it actually often signals accuracy in having interpreted the organization's needs. By dealing with the resistance directly, audit teams can work through barriers to implementing process improvements.

What Are the Signs of Resistance?

In many cases, resistance may be expressed directly. Direct objections to recommendations are relatively easy to address, inasmuch as they can be discussed and resolved. When recommendations are being presented, team members should stop frequently to allow those who are listening to the report to voice any objections or disagreements. Those who are presenting the data should be careful not to become defensive or to punish those who express reservations about the recommendations. It is impossible to deal with objections unless they are voiced; therefore, the audit team should welcome the expression of objections or differences of opinion. The following tips may be used for surfacing and dealing with direct resistance:

• Provide many opportunities for others to express their concerns.

• Carefully clarify any confusing concerns.

• Deal with important or easy concerns immediately. Defer the remainder.

• Summarize the concerns before moving on. Show that concerns have been heard.

• It may even be helpful to list concerns on a flip chart or blackboard.

If direct resistance continues, the following steps may be necessary:

• Talk about the differences of opinion.

• Voice concern and support for negotiating a resolution.

• Avoid struggles for control of the situation.

Dealing with Indirect Resistance

In other cases, resistance may be subtle and elusive. Indirect resistance is difficult to identify and deal with because its manifestations seem logical. People who are experiencing indirect resistance may feel that they are "getting the run around." Many different forms of resistance may manifest themselves in a single meeting:

• Request for more detail.

• Providing too much detail in response to questions.

• Complaining that there isn't enough time to implement recommendations.

• Claiming that the recommendations are impractical.

• Attacking those who propose improvement initiatives.

• Acting confused.

• Responding with silence.

• Intellectualizing about the data.

• Moralizing that problems wouldn't exist if it weren't for "those people".

• Agreeing to implement recommendations with no intention of acting on them.

• Asking questions about methodology.

• Arguing that previous problems have resolved themselves.

• Focusing on solutions before findings are fully understood.

Almost any of these responses is legitimate in moderate amounts. For example, members of the group may have concerns about the audit's methodology that should be considered. Managers may realistically wonder where they will find the time to implement recommendations. However, if refusal to act on recommendations persists once legitimate concerns have been addressed, then the audit team is probably facing indirect resistance.

Many models used in sales training provide recommendations for overcoming resistance. These methods suggest the use of data and logical arguments to win the point and convince the other person to buy whatever is being sold. These models work well for direct resistance. However, indirect resistance is normally based on feelings rather than logic. Therefore, the only way to truly overcome resistance is to deal with the emotional processes that cause it to happen in the first place. It is almost impossible to talk people out of the way they feel.

Feelings pass and change when they are expressed directly. A key skill for audit teams that are attempting to implement recommendations is to ask the people who are presenting resistance to put directly into words what they are experiencing. The most effective way to make this happen is for the audit team members to address directly what is happening in the situation. The following keys provide help in surfacing and dealing with indirect resistance.

- *Work once or twice with the person's concern, even when it feels as if he or she is resisting recommendations.*

By attempting to work with the problem stated by the person raising a concern, audit team members can determine whether the concern is legitimate or whether it is an excuse for not taking action. If the issues raised are legitimate, the person should show some willingness to discuss and resolve them. If the issues are manifestations of indirect resistance, the person will probably respond with other forms of resistance.

- *Identify the form the resistance is taking.*

Paying attention to the dynamics of a discussion can provide important clues as to whether or not a person is resisting recommendations. If a person is consistently distancing him or herself from those who are presenting the audit findings, using gestures or postures that suggest tension or discomfort, while at the same time presenting arguments for why the recommendations presented are inappropriate, it is probably a sign of resistance. The non-verbal responses of the presenters may also signal the onset of resistance. If presenters feel that they are suppressing negative feelings or becoming bored or irritated, it may be further evidence that the client is resisting.

Once presenters become aware of the resistance, the next step is to put it into words. This is best done by using neutral, everyday language. The skill is to describe the form of the resistance in a way that encourages the person to make a more direct statement of the reservation he or she is experiencing.

One general rule for stating what type of resistance is being manifested is to phrase the statement in common, non-threatening language. Statements should be made in the same tone and language that would be used to address a problem with a spouse or close friend. The statement should be made with as little evaluation as possible; it is the presenter's observation about what is happening in the situation.

A second general rule for surfacing indirect resistance involves not talking for a couple of moments after the presenter has stated what he or she has observed. There may be a temptation to elaborate on the observation, or to support it with evidence. However, continuing the statement will reduce the tension in the situation. Without tension, the person who is resisting feels no discomfort, and is unlikely to address the issue directly. Moreover, elaborating on the original statement may increase the other person's defensiveness and reduce the chances of solving the problem.

If stating the problem in direct, non-punishing terms fails to bring the resistance out into the open, there may be little more the audit team can do to overcome the indirect resistance. The best strategy in this case is to avoid resisting the resistance. Team members should support the person who is resisting and proceed with the implementation of recommendations to the extent possible.

BUILDING AN ONGOING AUDIT PROGRAM

A s the pace of change increases, and as organization leaders become more and more committed to continuously improving their effectiveness and efficiency, audits of all types of processes will become more common. The most effective companies will establish programs of ongoing audits, whereby a number of goals can be accomplished:

• Performance improvements can be measured over time.

• Important changes in the company's environment can be systematically monitored.

• Managers can make a habit of change and improvement, rather than resisting it.

• Those areas that are of highest importance to the company can be routinely improved.

• Processes can be modified to be in alignment with changes in strategy or in the environment.

As with all management techniques, however, an enduring program of ongoing audits requires that audits become integrated into the overall management system. The following guidelines are keys to weaving audits into the fabric of day-to-day operations.

Establish Support for Ongoing Audits

W hile support for audits begins at the executive level, ownership for the audit process must be felt throughout the organization if an ongoing program is to be successful. The following actions will help to broaden support for the audit process, while ensuring greater benefit from the audit.

• *Share the results of the audit with everyone throughout the organization.*

By keeping others informed about the results of an audit, managers reassure those who participate in and are affected by the audit of the integrity of the process. Employees sometimes become suspicious of probing investigators; they may have doubts about how the information will be used, or whether the information will be used. By sharing audit results, managers make an implicit commitment to improving the processes that have been evaluated.

• *Act on the audit results.*

Questions will be raised about continuing audits if early assessments bear no fruits. Failing to act on performance gaps that are identified leads to cynicism and lack of trust among those who work with the problems daily. On the other hand, improving a process can create the momentum that comes from accomplishment. Committing resources and attention to the improvement opportunities revealed by an audit also shows management commitment to the improvement process.

• *Let others know when performance has improved.*

Communicating the positive results from an audit is one way of rewarding the people who contributed to that improvement. It also builds faith in the effectiveness of the audit process. Moreover, showing that performance has improved is another means of reassuring people of a commitment to the improvement process.

• *Reward people for their part in improvements.*

Increasing efficiency and effectiveness can often be a threatening experience for those who are involved in a work process. Improving the way resources are used often means eliminating the need for some of the people who have been involved in the process. Although flatter, leaner organizations often preclude the possibility of offering promotions, managers should nevertheless attempt to ensure that people who contribute to performance improvement find their own situations better rather than worse as a result.

Rewards for helping to close performance gaps may span a range from thanking people for their efforts to planning a group celebration to offering bonuses or pay increases for improvement. Rewards are especially meaningful when people are allowed to suggest what rewards they would like for their contribution. This may provide managers with new ideas for rewards that may be less costly to the organization than financial recognition.

• *Involve a wide variety of people in the audit process.*

People can be involved in the audit process in many ways. By involving people from a broad spectrum, more people learn about audit techniques and results, thus spreading commitment to the audit process throughout the organization. By involving many people in the data-gathering process, employees feel that action plans growing out of the audit were a result of their input. Excluding people from the data-gathering phase usually reduces the feeling of ownership for the results, thus making people feel as if initiatives are being imposed on them. By the same token, involving a broad range of people in the development of action plans expands ownership for the plans and allows for the generation of more ideas.

Part 3

Implementing
a Corporate
Identity Audit:
Questions and Checklists

This part of the *Corporate Identity Audit* comprises a series of questions based on the nine steps given in the section *Steps in Performing an Identity Audit*, plus some follow-up questions relating to ongoing management of the identity program. All of these questions have been designed to help you plan and implement your audit in a straightforward and practical manner, covering all the relevant parts of the audit in the correct sequence.

NINE STEPS TO AUDITING CORPORATE IDENTITY

- Step 1 Select the Audit Team
- Step 2 Assess Key Elements in the Corporate Identity
- Step 3 Determine Who Should Be Interviewed
- Step 4 Conduct Audit Interviews
- Step 5 Audit Corporate Identity Factors
- Step 6 Summarize Salient Points
- Step 7 Determine the Options for Change
- Step 8 Present the Audit Results
- Step 9 Use the Audit Data to Improve the Corporate Identity

Note: You may find that referring to the information both before and after the nine steps in *The Corporate Identity Audit* will help you to answer the questions that follow in this section, and thus carry out your own internal audit. Additionally, useful background information is given below before each set of questions.

SELECT THE
AUDIT TEAM

BACKGROUND INFORMATION

The audit team must have enough influence to ensure that corporate identity is seen as an important issue throughout the organization. The audit team may consist of individuals with expertise in:

- sales and marketing
- communications
- operations
- construction management
- engineering
- design.

The team composition will vary depending upon the nature of your company. The "Questions" section below will help you to determine what is right for you.

QUESTIONS

- Might audit team members include senior level executives and/or middle managers with expertise in:
  - ❑ sales and marketing
  - ❑ marketing research
  - ❑ communications
  - ❑ operations
  - ❑ engineering
  - ❑ industrial design
  - ❑ graphic design?

Note: Corporate identity audit team members may be segmented into smaller interview groups to expedite the process and to pair appropriate levels, backgrounds and expertise with each intended audience/group/individual being interviewed.

- Will the scope of work carried out by the team include:
  - ❏ investigating how the company is perceived
  - ❏ determining why the company is perceived in this way
  - ❏ agreeing (if possible) on how the company should be perceived
  - ❏ deciding how to create that perception?

- Will the team first prepare a written brief that describes the task?

- Will this brief be comprehensive and take into account its parameters in terms of:
  - ❏ strategy
  - ❏ marketing
  - ❏ communication
  - ❏ behavior?

- Will a short version of this brief be circulated to senior and middle management?

- If appropriate, will the senior or middle management cascade the brief down to their own departments?

- Will a variation of the brief also be circulated to selected external audiences?

Note: An example of what a brief should cover is shown on the first page of Step 1 in the section *Steps in Performing an Identity Audit*.

Once the brief has been distributed, the team can begin its work, which will consist primarily of interviewing appropriate individuals inside and outside the company. The questions that follow in Step 2 will help you to undertake this work.

ASSESS KEY ELEMENTS IN THE CORPORATE IDENTITY

BACKGROUND INFORMATION

The audit team must be clear about:

- the nature of the organization
- the key components of its corporate identity, and
- the ways in which the key components are projected.

This should take the form of two assessments:

Assessment 1, and

Assessment 2.

The questions below will help you with your work on these assessments.

QUESTIONS

Assessment 1

Note: The first assessment should consider the four areas in which corporate identity manifests itself (products and services – what is made or sold; environments – where products and services are made or sold; communications – how a company explains what it does; behavior – the way a company's people represent it to its public). This can be conducted by the audit team and relates to the descriptions in the second and third pages of the introduction in *The Corporate Identity Audit*.

- Will the audit team assess the importance of the company's main products and services in shaping the corporate identity?

- Will the audit team assess the importance of the company's location and physical environment in shaping the corporate identity?

- Will the audit team assess the importance of the way the company communicates in shaping the corporate identity?

- Will the audit team assess the importance of the people within the company in shaping the corporate identity?

- Will factors shaping the perceptions of financial analysts be considered?

- Does the way the organization is presented on television and in the press define public perceptions?

- If the answer to the previous question is "Yes", will attention be paid to the factors that influence the thinking of journalists about the company?

Note: A sample of this first assessment form along with two figures (Figure 4: Example Assessment Chart, and Figure 5: Completed Example Assessment Chart) are shown in Step 2 of the section *Steps in Performing an Identity Audit*.

Assessment 2

The second assessment should consider the three main categories of corporate identity (monolithic identity, endorsed identity and branded identity). This assessment can also be conducted by the audit team itself and with reference to the definitions given in the first and second pages of "Types of Corporate Identity" in *The Corporate Identity Audit*.

- Are senior management clear about the type of identity that the organization possesses?

- Considering the company's name, brands, advertising strategy, competition, presence in different international markets, and referring to the definitions of monolithic identity, endorsed identity and branded identity, will the team assess the importance of each category in the company's overall identity?

- In completing this assessment, will most attention be paid to the perceptions of customers and/or the general public, since the financial community will inevitably have a stronger awareness of the corporate whole than of individual brands?

Note: A sample of this second assessment form along with two figures (Figure 6: Example Assessment Chart, and Figure 7: Completed Example Assessment Chart) are shown in Step 2 of the section *Steps in Performing an Identity Audit*. If the assessment form proves difficult to complete, it's also worth noting that a more complex breakdown of the types of corporate identity is shown in Figure 12, Step 6.

Having assessed key elements in corporate identity, the next important step is to determine who should be interviewed. You can do this by looking at the questions below, which relate to Step 3 of this audit.

DETERMINE WHO SHOULD BE INTERVIEWED

BACKGROUND INFORMATION

Data needs to be gathered from a variety of sources both inside and outside the company. You will therefore need to talk to a range of people using both:

1 internal interviews, and

2 external interviews.

The questions below relate to both types of interview.

QUESTIONS

1. Internal Interviews

- Will interviewees be selected from all levels and all parts of the company?

- Will interviewees make up an appropriate demographic mix?

- Will the heads of each division be interviewed?

- Will an appropriate number of middle managers and staff be interviewed?

- In selecting potential interviewees, will the audit team ensure that undue weight is not given to any particular area of the business?

- Are there likely to be political reasons why some internal audiences are included as interviewees?

- Will the interviewees include a small number of people who have worked for the company for a relatively short time (say 6–24 months)?

2. External Interviews

- Will the interviews be conducted with people representing:
  - ❏ journalists
  - ❏ suppliers
  - ❏ competitors

❏ collaborators

❏ customers?

Note: In order to ensure that no significant group has been excluded from your audit, refer to the list under the subhead "Audiences", which appears in *The Role of Vision in Corporate Identity* in *The Corporate Identity Audit.*

• Will the audit team ensure a balance in selecting interviewees?

• Will customers be chosen at random, rather than from a list of "best customers" or from a list of those who have recently written to the company?

• Will the audit team talk to customers of competitors to find out why they don't buy from your company?

Note: Each audit – internal and external – usually requires that about 30 people be interviewed, although the number will vary according to:

• the size of the company

• the number of its units

• the diversity of the units.

Having considered the options for internal and external interviewees, the next few questions relate to how to proceed from this point.

• Will a list of interviewees, both internal and external, be compiled and cross-checked by different members of the team, canvassing among their senior colleagues?

• Will it be necessary to reassure some internal interviewees that their responses will not be attributed to them individually but rather documented collectively?

• Will it be necessary to reassure some internal interviewees that their answers will not be taken in any way to reflect upon their current performance or future prospects?

• Will it be made clear to all interviewees that there are no right or wrong answers?

• Will it be made clear to all interviewees that all interviews are confidential?

Once the list of people to be interviewed is completed, the audit team is ready to begin its research. The next section asks a series of questions that will enable the team to do this in the most effective way.

CONDUCT
AUDIT
INTERVIEWS

BACKGROUND INFORMATION

The research phase of the audit involves interviewing and systematically examining the physical representations of the company's identity.

The "Questions" section below will help you with the following.

1 The main objective of the interviews.

2 The range of questions.

3 Internal interviews.

4 Internal interviewing techniques.

5 External interviews.

6 External interview techniques.

You will also find extensive sample questions which can be asked during internal and external interviews.

QUESTIONS

1. The Main Objectives of the Interviews

- Will the main objectives cover:
    - ❏ how much people know about the company
    - ❏ what opinions or judgments they attract to their knowledge of the company
    - ❏ how clear and consistent those opinions and judgments are
    - ❏ how far those opinions and judgments vary from the identity which senior managers wish to project?

2. The Range of Questions

- For both internal and external interviewees, will the range of questions cover the four areas of corporate identity:
    - ❏ products/services
    - ❏ environments

- ❏ communications

- ❏ behavior?

- Will the nature of the industry/sector in which your organization operates be addressed in the course of the interview?

- Will the issues here include:

  - ❏ industry/sector size

  - ❏ growth patterns

  - ❏ rates of change

  - ❏ competitiveness

  - ❏ use of technology

  - ❏ environmental concerns

  - ❏ corporate culture

  - ❏ profitability?

- Will the organization itself be addressed in the course of the interview?

- Will the issues here include:

  - ❏ size

  - ❏ position

  - ❏ profitability

  - ❏ market share

  - ❏ competitiveness

  - ❏ quality

  - ❏ advertising

  - ❏ environmental responsibility?

- Will brand, businesses and divisions be addressed in the course of the interview?

- Will the interviews seek to establish whether the internal perception of the type of corporate identity is matched in reality by external perceptions?

3. Internal Interviews

- Will the responses of internal interviewees be heavily conditioned by their:
  - ❏ role
  - ❏ responsibility
  - ❏ length of service with the company?

4. Internal Interviewing Techniques

- Will the interview be:
  - ❏ informal
  - ❏ confidential
  - ❏ loosely structured?

- Although interviewers must be clear about the issues to be dealt with, will they be careful not to follow a set written questionnaire too closely?

Below is a list of suggested questions for the Corporate Identity Audit internal interview. These questions should be tailored to suit the particular make-up, market and operating environment of the company.

- How long have you been with the company?

- What did you do before you worked here?

- What is your position/responsibility in the company?

- Have your perceptions of the company changed since you began to work here?

- What were your perceptions before working here?

- What are they now?

- Would you associate any of the following image attributes with your company:
  - ❏ innovative
  - ❏ friendly
  - ❏ progressive
  - ❏ formal
  - ❏ conservative
  - ❏ futuristic
  - ❏ dependable
  - ❏ trustworthy
  - ❏ national/regional/international
  - ❏ responsive

- How would you describe your company and its products/services to friends or strangers who asked?

- In your opinion, is your company understood by outsiders as you understand it?

  If not, what is the difference in the way outside people view the organization?

- How would you describe the products and services your company offers to someone in your industry?

- Who do you believe are your company's major competitors?
  (Please rank 1, 2, 3, etc.)

- Do you see an opportunity for your own personal growth with the company?

  Why or why not?

- Where do you see the company's opportunities for growth?

  How?

  Why?

- What barriers are preventing the company from achieving the growth you described?

- What is your opinion of the current corporate identity used by the company?

- What does the current symbol/signature/trademark suggest to you?

  Do you think it reflects the personality and long-term mission of the company?

  Why or why not?

- What colors do you associate with the company?

- What are the major strengths and weaknesses of the company in general, i.e., what does the company do best?

- What are the major strengths and weaknesses of the products/services of the company?

- If there were one important message you wanted to deliver to the CEO of the company, what would that be?

- In what ways do you think the company could communicate better to its diverse publics?

Brands:

- It is my understanding that each brand manager runs his/her own area. Do you believe this structure is appropriate today? Should they have more or less autonomy and why?

- What visual relationship should the company's branded products and services have to the parent company or division?

Note: It will be necessary to retain a balance of closed and open questions. Closed questions will help to put the interviewee at ease and collect information that can be compared accurately. Open questions may lead the interviewer into new and unsuspected areas.

- Will the interviewer start by explaining that the meeting is part of a research project, and that this, together with all other interviews, is confidential?
- Will the interviewer then ask questions that get on to a personal note?

Note: This "warm-up" part of the meeting is important because it:

- ❏ helps both parties to get to know each other
- ❏ gives the interviewees a sense of their own significance
- ❏ enables the interviewer to get some idea of the person being questioned.

- Will the interviewer be mindful not to discourage a stream of anecdotes and unstructured reminiscences?

Note: The object is to gain the confidence of the interviewee so that all the issues are discussed quite freely and without reserve or caution.

- Will the interviewer sometimes be challenging or act as devil's advocate, by asking questions such as:
  - ❏ "I understand that the company is run by a strong CEO; do you believe the CEO should have more or less control and why?"
  - ❏ "Besides the CEO or chairman, who else is known for making key decisions?"
  - ❏ "What is the company especially good at and is this well-known to outside audiences?"
  - ❏ "Is it good at marketing or manufacturing or cost control?"
  - ❏ "In what areas does the company need improvement and is this well-known to outside audiences?"
  - ❏ "Which is the best company in the whole business?"
  - ❏ "In other words, which of your competitors do you most fear?"?

Note: Each interview should last from 30 to 60 minutes in length. In some cases, a second or follow-up interview may be necessary.

5. External Interviews

- Will external interviews find out how much outsiders know about the mechanics of the company in terms of:
  - ❏ size
  - ❏ profitability
  - ❏ ownership
  - ❏ primary products
  - ❏ services
  - ❏ divisions?

- Will external interviews find out the views of outsiders relating to the company's:
  - ❏ strengths
  - ❏ weaknesses
  - ❏ impact on the outside world?

- Will external interviews find out what overall perceptions outsiders have about the organization?

- Depending on the audit team's evaluations at Step 2, will questions need to take close account of the different types of corporate identity and the key factors at work?

- Will the questions check whether external perceptions of, say, the importance of brands and staff behavior match the perceptions of the internal interviewees?

- Will the questions establish in greater detail the interviewee's feelings and opinions on these factors?

6. External Interview Techniques

- Will a flexible structure for interview with a good mix of open and closed questions be adopted?

Below is a list of suggested questions for the Corporate Identity Audit external interview which would be suitable for customers, suppliers, the general public and journalists.

- What is your relationship to the company?

- How familiar would you say you are with the company? (Prompt? Very familiar? Somewhat familiar? Not at all familiar?)

- How would you describe what the company does?

  What specific brand name products/services does it offer?

- Do you believe the company is a regional, national or international organization?

- Who do you believe are the primary competitors of the company?

- Based on your own experiences or based on what you have heard or read, would you rate the company's overall reputation as excellent, good, fair or poor?

- When you hear the name of the company, what things come to mind?

- Why do you do business with the company?

- Would you recommend this company's products/services to a friend?

  Why or why not?

- Can you recall or describe any advertising the company has done recently?

  How did it influence your perception of the company?

- Could you recognize the company's annual report among others on a crowded coffee table?

- What symbol and colors come to mind when you hear the company's name?

- Would you associate any of the following words (image attributes) with the company:
  - ❑ innovative   ❑ friendly   ❑ progressive   ❑ formal
  - ❑ conservative   ❑ futuristic   ❑ dependable   ❑ trustworthy
  - ❑ national/regional/international   ❑ responsive

- If the company came out with a new product or service, would you/your own company be a primary sales target?

  If so, why?

- How would you rate this company's products/services on a scale of one to five when compared to the competition?

- How would this company's products be viewed in other countries in terms of product quality and image, on a scale of one to five, five being high quality and image; one being low quality and image?

- Is it important for you to know the company who makes the branded products and services you buy?

  Do you think the company's name should be clearly communicated along with the brand name?

- How would you rate the company's sales literature in presenting an image that is clear and consistent with the company's desired positioning?

Below are questions for the Corporate Identity Audit external interview which present more in-depth business-related areas of discussion for financial analysts and outside consultants such as the company's advertising agency or public relations firm.

Nature of the industry
- Is it a high growth/low growth industry?

- Is it going through rapid technological/marketing development or is it stable?

- Is it, or will it become, highly competitive?

- Is it converging into a few groups?

- Is it threatened by environmental or other external considerations?

- Is it intrinsically a capital/labor-intensive business?

The company
- Is the company well positioned/badly positioned in the market place?

- How big is its market share?

- How profitable is it?

- How many people does it employ?

- Is the employment vs profitability figure good or bad by industry standards?

- Who are its main competitors?

- How does each of the major players compare in terms of:
  - ❏ size
  - ❏ profitability

- ❏ geographic spread
- ❏ product range
- ❏ product quality
- ❏ innovation/technology
- ❏ marketing
- ❏ public image
- ❏ known brand names?

- What is the long-term vision of the company?

- Is the management good enough to execute it?

- On the whole has the business improved or deteriorated in the last five years? What sort of business will it be in five years' time?

- Will it occupy its present position, or will it be stronger/weaker?

- Is there an admired model within the industry?

- Who is it?

- How is it better/worse than our company in terms of:
  - ❏ marketing
  - ❏ technology
  - ❏ sales
  - ❏ product quality
  - ❏ service
  - ❏ distribution?

- Do the following make it an admired model:
  - ❏ image
  - ❏ long history in the market
  - ❏ market share?

Brands

- Is the company known mainly through its corporate name — or its brand names?

- What are the main brand names?

- Do most respondents know most brand names or are most people only familiar with the brands with which they deal?

- How does the company articulate the relationship between brand names and corporate names?

Note: External audiences generally have less time to spend in an interview than the company's employees. The suggested length, which should be stated upfront when scheduling the interview, is 15–20 minutes.

Having worked through the questions relating to internal and external interviews, both in terms of how the interviews should be conducted and the questions that should be asked, it is time to audit the corporate identity factors. The questions below, which relate to Step 5, will help you to do this.

AUDIT CORPORATE IDENTITY FACTORS

BACKGROUND INFORMATION

The relative weightings allocated in Step 2 to the key elements of corporate identity will have been confirmed or revised as a result of the internal and external interviews. The audit team now needs to conduct an independent review of these elements, as follows.

1 Products, services and environments.

2 Communication.

3 Behavior.

Note: This review can take place at the same time as the interviews. It is essential that a talented and professional designer serve on the audit team which evaluates all visual communications.

The questions that follow are related to each of these elements in turn.

QUESTIONS

1. Products, Services and Environments

- Will the audit team review:
  - ❑ proposals
  - ❑ billheads
  - ❑ letterheads
  - ❑ business cards
  - ❑ envelopes
  - ❑ advertising formats
  - ❑ promotional items
  - ❑ internal publications
  - ❑ memo forms
  - ❑ labels on packages, letters, etc.
  - ❑ shipping containers
  - ❑ gummed tape

❑ name plates

❑ embossing dies and stamps used on products

❑ rubber stamps for check endorsement, mail receiving, etc.

❑ production and cost control forms

❑ master forms

❑ name tags

❑ press release letterheads

❑ vehicles?

Note: These are all pertinent items from the corporate identity checklist.

• Will the audit team assemble appropriate samples from each department, division, unit or site?

• Will the audit team also collect products of packaging materials, where appropriate?

• Will the team visit and photograph, if necessary, different buildings, sites, showrooms, stores and offices?

• Will attention be paid to both the internal and the external appearance?

• Will examples and photographs of all appropriate symbols be collected, reviewed and checked for coherence in visual presentation and quality?

• Will this collection be carefully catalogued to highlight inconsistencies, which may be considerable?

2. Communication

• Will the audit team consider how the organization deals with it own audiences through:

❑ public relations

❑ annual reports

❑ display and TV advertising

❑ other formal and informal channels?

Note: For further information, see the corporate communications checklist, which is shown in Figure 11 in Step 5.

- Does the group always describe itself consistently?

- Does a coherent message emerge?

- Is there a clear organizational chart and is the company's structure reflected properly in the corporate identity and visual communications material put forth?

- Should it be?

Additional questions which may be asked in this context can be broken into those relating to internal communications and those relating to the media. These questions are listed below.

Internal Communications

- How does the organization communicate with its employees and, where appropriate, with other quasi-internal audiences?

- Does it have regular videos or newsletters?

- How many?

- How often?

- Aimed at which audiences?

- Controlled by whom?

- Are these top down or bottom up?

- Is the general quality good or poor?

Media

- What do TV and the press say about the company?

- How often is it in the news and in what context?

- What formal and informal media and public relations activities does it undertake?

- Are these controlled centrally or by division?

- What is the relationship between brands and corporate communications?

- What is the relationship between marketing, advertising, and corporate communication departments?

Note: As part of the audit process, the technical and general media should be reviewed in order to see how the group and its activities are perceived.

3. Behavior

- Does the audit team already have access to a considerable body of survey material in the form of customer opinion/satisfaction research?

- If such surveys are not conducted regularly, or recent results are not available, will a customer program be instituted?

- Alternatively, might the audit team wish to include additional questions in existing survey/opinion-gathering forms and questionnaires?

Note: In this part of the audit, it will be important to remember that it is consistency which is being measured. Customer Satisfaction surveys, however, will pay more attention to improvement or deterioration in reported perceptions of employee behavior. For this reason, the Corporate Identity audit team may need to go back to the raw data from previous surveys to analyze the different response from different locations.

Questions on behavioral perceptions should include the four that follow.

- What are the different parts of the organization like to deal with?

- Are representatives of the company polite or rude?

- How quickly are customers served or telephone calls answered and transferred?

- How helpful are staff in answering questions and resolving problems?

Note: During Step 5 of the audit, which should take only about two months unless completely new research has to be undertaken, the audit team should meet regularly to compare notes.

Once the audit of corporate identity factors has taken place, and having already undertaken a series of interviews, the next step in the audit is to summarize the salient points. The questions below, which relate to Step 6, will help you to do this.

SUMMARIZE SALIENT POINTS

BACKGROUND INFORMATION

During the interviews, certain critical points will have emerged. These will enable auditors to address important issues (as listed below) in assessing corporate identity, and will lead to consensus-building within the organization.

1 Why are we perceived in this way?

2 Why is the organization misunderstood?

3 Uncovering issues.

The "Questions" section below will help you to look at each of these three areas in turn.

QUESTIONS

1. Why Are We Perceived in this Way?

Note: Further information related to this question can be found by studying the definitions of the three basic types of corporate identity (which can be found in the first and second pages of "Types of Corporate Identity" in *The Corporate Identity Audit*). Figure 12 in Step 6 shows three additional ways of subdividing these types.

- Will the audit team carry out an identity program through the disciplines of corporate strategy, marketing, communication and organizational behavior?

Corporate Strategy

- Does this include the company's mission/vision, long-term and short-term business objectives?

- Does corporate identity reflect and communicate what the company stands for?

Marketing

- Does corporate identity support the company's marketing objectives?

- Does corporate identity distinguish the company from the competition?

- Does corporate identity position the company appropriately in the minds of its key publics?

Communication

- Do all communications clearly convey the corporate identity?

Organizational Behavior

- Can the company create and sustain a work environment that encourages employees to achieve the corporate mission and to project a positive image in all endeavors to further enhance the corporate identity?

Note: By using this framework, the audit team can assess the critical factors that affect its identity and discover clues that will help them to know how the company is perceived.

2. Why is the Organization Misunderstood?

- If the reasons why an organization is misunderstood are not clear once research has been completed, will the team examine the identity of the organization to determine where there are anomalies, gaps, and contradictions that lead to misconceptions about the company's identity?

Note: This examination can be carried out using all of the tools outlined under the subhead "Why Are We Perceived in this Way?", which appears earlier in Step 6 in the section *Steps in Performing an Identity Audit.*

- Does the company have an identity that is:
  - ❑ monolithic
  - ❑ thematic
  - ❑ dual
  - ❑ endorsed
  - ❑ conditional
  - ❑ decentralized/branded
  - ❑ some combination of these?

Note: If some parts of the organization are monolithic, others endorsed and still others branded, it may not be surprising that audiences are confused.

- How does the mix of strategy, communication, marketing and organizational behavior affect the way the organization is perceived?

Note: The audit team will probably come across examples of inconsistency in communications, presentation, behavior and strategy. When these inconsistencies are looked at as a whole, they usually explain why there are misconceptions about the size, scope and values of the company.

3. Uncovering Issues

- Will the identity audit uncover issues familiar to some individuals within the organization, but that have not been considered in terms of their impact on the identity?

- Is it likely that the early stages of the audit will have opened up other interesting and significant issues?

- For example, might there be:
  - ❑ inconsistencies in presentation
  - ❑ waste and duplication in purchasing
  - ❑ sales and communication overlaps
  - ❑ contradictions and missed opportunities in human resource management?

- In particular, might the disciplines of corporate strategy, organizational behavior, communication and marketing (and the links or lack of links between them, and the reasons for this) be exposed in this part of the audit?

Having undertaken this part of the audit, the team should now explore the differences between how the company is perceived by various audiences and how it would like to be perceived. Questions that will facilitate this information are listed below.

DETERMINE THE OPTIONS FOR CHANGE

BACKGROUND INFORMATION

Determining the "how" and "why" of establishing an appropriate identity will require ideas from beyond the audit team. The implications of what has been found should be examined by a broader group. Regardless of the results of the first two stages of the audit, the team must consider why the company is perceived as it is, and what should be done to change that perception if it is not in line with what the company wants to project.

The "Questions" section below will help to ascertain this.

QUESTIONS

- When an organization or parts of an organization are presented in an inconsistent, unclear, or contradictory fashion, will the overall vision of the company be more clearly articulated?

Note: In such cases, the vision has faded, was never clear in the first place, or has not taken into account changes within the company and its market place.

- Will the audit team clarify the company's current identity and press for a consideration of the company's vision?

- Will the vision answer the questions:
  - ❏ "What drives our business?"
  - ❏ "Are we a business whose heart lies in technological excellence?"
  - ❏ "Are we a business whose heart lies in understanding the consumer?"
  - ❏ "Are we a business whose heart lies in developing new products and introducing them to the market?"
  - ❏ "Do we have another priority?"?

Note: The company's vision is further articulated in Step 9 in the section *Steps in Performing an Identity Audit*.

- Will the audit team start a dialog on the subject of identity and the factors that contribute to the company's current identity?

- Each time a change takes place within the company, will top executives be presented with design decisions concerning:
  - ❏ names
  - ❏ trademarks
  - ❏ letterheads, etc.?

- Will decisions relating to these be made independently of previous decisions?

- Are key executives speaking the same language to a common end?

- Are these executives communicating with each other?

Note: These key executives are notably:
  - ❏ the public relations director
  - ❏ the marketing manager
  - ❏ the advertising manager
  - ❏ the sales manager
  - ❏ the purchasing agent
  - ❏ the president.

- When viewed all together, does the visual output project a dynamic, organized company on the way up with solid foundations?

- Or does it make the company look like a gangling adolescent, all arms and legs, each going in a different direction?

- Does the company look like it is having a hard time trying to form a cohesive family organization that works as a team?

- Does it look like the executives have confidence in their positions on the team?

- Does the company look its age?

- Do visual materials look old, tired and inflexible?

- Is the graphic control system an exercise in rigidity?

- Is "status quo thinking" settling in over management?

- Is the firm promoting a look of corporate sterility or stagnation instead of corporate synergy and dynamism?

- Are the products and services dressed to travel?

- Will they be welcomed in other countries?

- Do they need a new trademark, trade name, and trade dress?

Note: Detailed discussion examples for use in clarifying the company vision are given in Step 7 in the section *Steps in Performing an Identity Audit*.

The development of an effective corporate identity program will rest on the effectiveness of presenting the findings of the audit. The questions that follow will help the audit team to present its analysis, along with the issues and implications that they see growing out of the identity audit, to the appropriate people for considerations.

PRESENT THE AUDIT RESULTS

BACKGROUND INFORMATION

All of the points previously discussed in this audit, including the development of a new vision, are legitimate aspects of the work of the team. All have relevance to its findings and all are critical to improving corporate performance.

Answering the questions below will help teams to present all of their audit results.

QUESTIONS

- Does the audit team clearly understand the strategic options available to the organization in terms of corporate/brand identity?

- Should the team be trying to discover which strategic option each audience perceives as best for the organization?

- Will the team show to board members visual examples which demonstrate the potential corporate identity options?

- Will these visual examples help to focus the board's decision on the audit results?

Note: If board members are persuaded that the corporate identity is in need of attention and development, they may now seek the assistance of outside consultants to develop and implement and program.

Most companies fail to manage their identity actively and effectively. This section of the audit concludes by posing a series of questions below, which may help to provide ideas for using the identity as a powerful management tool.

Use the Audit Data to Improve the Corporate Identity

BACKGROUND INFORMATION

In most cases, the implementation of an identity program will require the help of outside consultants, and will follow the sequence below.

1 Setting up the identity structure.

2 Establishing the working party.

3 Developing and articulating the vision.

4 Identity program launch and introduction.

5 Program implementation: cost and time schedules.

The "Questions" section that follows will help you to deal with the first four parts of this sequence.

QUESTIONS

1. Setting Up the Identity Structure

- Will the corporate identity program be managed at both the top and the middle levels of the organization?

- Will there be commitment to the program from the board and the CEO?

- Will the program be spearheaded/led by a senior executive from marketing or corporate communications, who will be given the appropriate authority and access to resources, and work directly with the CEO on the program?

- Will it be helpful if the executive in charge of the program has a marketing or communications background?

2. Establishing the Working Party

- Will the working party represent those parts of the company that will be most affected by the program?

- In particular, will there be representation from:
  - ❏ corporate strategy
  - ❏ marketing
  - ❏ communications
  - ❏ organizational behaviour?

- Will purchasing, legal and technical people also be available to lend their expertise?

- With the CEO, will the working party attempt to determine the scope of the corporate identity program?

Note: Sometimes it may be useful if the working party reports to a small, senior-level steering committee.

3. Developing and Articulating the Vision

- Will the issue of vision be fully addressed at this point?

- Will the vision be based both upon the reality of the organization and on what it believes it can realistically become?

Note: Each company is unique: each has unique strengths that can be clearly articulated. No company should attempt to copy its competitors, so each corporate vision will be unique.

- Will the vision be projected in a form that all audiences of the organization can see and understand intuitively and immediately?

Note: Just as the existing corporate identity was measured in terms of written and oral communication, behavior and visual presentation, so the vision will be communicated in these ways.

- Is it appropriate to change the symbol if a new corporate identity program is launched?

- Or will modification of the symbol be more appropriate?

Note: Organizations that have spent millions on promoting their existing symbols over a period of years are more likely to wish to modify what they have rather than change it completely. However, there are also situations when it is desirable to make a clean break and produce a new visual symbol. See the text under the subhead "Developing and Articulating the Vision" and also Figures 15 and 16 in Step 9 of the section *Steps in Performing an Identity Audit*.

- If leaders of an organization decide to change the company's symbol, will a new visual identity be developed in conjunction with consultants or professionals involved in the project?

- Should they produce a series of possible visual approaches applied to a range of corporate activities?

Note: Eventually, one of these approaches will be chosen and developed so that it can be integrated into the visible manifestations of the company and its brands.

4. Identity Program Launch and Introduction

- Are people inside the company committed to, and informed about, the new identity before it emerges publicly?

Note: It is essential that the internal launch of an identity program takes place before the external launch.

- At the internal launch, will the corporate vision on which the identity is based be explained clearly and simply?

- Will the place of the vision as part of the company's philosophy be demonstrated?

- Will the commitment of management to drive home the vision through communication and behavior as well as through the new visual program be emphasized?

- Will it be explained at the internal launch that this visual part of the identity is simply the means by which the corporate vision is communicated?

- Will the external launch involve:
  - ❏ advertising
  - ❏ brochures
  - ❏ sales meetings
  - ❏ a press relations drive?

- If the company has a dealer organization, will the external launch be divided into two stages:
  - ❏ first, the dealer and special customer launch
  - ❏ second, a public launch?

Finally, the questions below address some of the issues of rolling out the corporate identity program, and keeping it running.

ONGOING MANAGEMENT OF THE IDENTITY PROGRAM

BACKGROUND INFORMATION

Having completed Steps 1 to 9, there are some other aspects of the corporate environment that also need to be taken into consideration in rolling out the corporate identity program. One of the most important of these is ensuring that it has adequate funding and is supported by adequate authority. Some of the variables to be taken into account are outlined through the questions below.

QUESTIONS

- Who is going to pay for the program: the center or the operating units?

- How should liaison between the company's different subsidiaries and geographic divisions and the central identity resource work?

- How should the resource be staffed and how many people should it have?

- Where should it be located?

- What are the lines of responsibility?

- How should the roles of the different disciplines (strategy, marketing, communication and organizational behavior) be co-ordinated?

There is always a danger that after the excitement of the investigation, design and launch work, continuing attention to the identity program will be neglected. Implementation is essentially a long-term process. The two questions that follow address the issues of what to expect once the program is in place.

- Will the logistics of the program take into account the changing priorities and requirements of the corporation as a whole?

- Will the working party, or another appropriate group, meet regularly (perhaps every two months) to review progress on the identity and to arbitrate when necessary between the differing interests within the organization?

Note: Suggestions for a small-scale identity program and the benefits of a corporate identity program are covered in detail. These sections follow on from the nine steps of the audit itself.

IN CONCLUSION ...

All of the questions listed in this section will hopefully help you to plan an audit that will allow for the regular re-evaluation of perceptions of the organization by its important audiences, and for the re-formulation or re-establishment of the company's vision when it has been forgotten or become outdated. The extensive explanations in the section entitled *Steps in Performing an Identity Audit* will help you to answer these questions to best effect.

Good luck!

Part 1: **Wally Olins** *is co-founder and Chairman of Wolff Olins in London. He is a leading authority on identity and has advised chief executives of many organizations, including Midland Bank, Forte, Akzo, Halifax, Renault, BT and ICI.* **Elinor Selame** *is president of BrandEquity International, a Massachusetts-based consulting firm whose clients include Kodak, Amoco, Haworth, Raytheon, General Cinema, IBM, Levi-Strauss and Bank of Boston. An internationally recognized expert on corporate identity and visual communications strategies, she has authored three books on identity and currently serves as president of the Package Design Council International.* **Part 2** *has been adapted from* The Company AuditGuide *published by Cambridge Strategy Publications Ltd.* **Part 3** *has been developed by Cambridge Strategy Publications Ltd.*